The Forgotten Child:
"If She Is Special, What Am I?"

The Forgotten Child: "If She Is Special, What Am I?"

Sibling Issues: When Learning Disabilities Cause Tension in the Home

by

ANNE FORD
AND
JOHN-RICHARD THOMPSON

ISBN-13: 9780692390306

TABLE OF CONTENTS

INTRODUCTION
"WHAT ABOUT ME?"

I have never enjoyed public speaking. I have gotten better at it, but when I first started, I would get so nervous I could barely hold my notes. After my first book *Laughing Allegra* was published, I was asked to go out on a book tour. I had recently stepped down as Chairman of the National Center for Learning Disabilities (NCLD). In that role, I had a great deal of exposure to some of the top experts in the field of learning disabilities. I knew all about latest medical research and government initiatives. I even did a little public speaking. Even so, I rarely found myself immersed in a group of fellow parents of children with LD. I often met with parents one-on-one at the NCLD offices but had few opportunities to talk with large groups until I began the book tour. For the first time, I found myself in the midst of mothers like myself, with the same concerns and fears and hopes for their children.

One of my first speaking engagements was in Dallas, Texas at a school for children with special needs. I was so nervous. I thought the speech might go well but dreaded the Question and Answer period. I worried someone might ask me a question I didn't understand or that I might not know the correct answer. My fears increased when I noticed a mother in distress. All during my speech she sat with tears rolling down her cheeks, and I assumed she might have experienced some very recent traumatic event — possibly that very morning. Instead, to my great surprise, she raised her hand and told us that the cause of all the angst and turmoil was her seeming inability to treat both her children equally. She felt like a neglectful parent and that she was not able to give her child without special needs the attention and time he deserved and the tears continued to flow when she asked what she could do about it.

I remember thinking, "My goodness, can it really be *that* bad?" If I'm honest about it, I also remember not having much to offer in the way of advice. I think I probably turned to one of the other mothers in the audience and asked if they had any suggestions. I simply had never considered sibling issues in such a serious way before.

I have since learned that, yes, it can really be that bad. The topic comes up so often in the Question and Answer period whenever I speak to parent groups that I usually incorporate it into my main speech in order to address this concern right away and give it the weight it deserves.

Sibling issues are not often thought of as one of the most urgent "crisis issues" when it comes to learning disabilities and related disorders — at least not at first. I define crisis issues as those such as the initial, sometimes shocking, diagnosis of LD; or trying to find the right help in school; or dealing with the mind-numbing, infuriating bureaucracy of the education system. Those issues demand immediate attention. They require action, even as they sometimes cause a debilitating sense of paralysis and indecision. They overwhelm and can become a parent's sole focus, with all other problems shrinking in comparison.

I know mothers (and was one myself) who experience the early years after a child's diagnosis with LD in a shell-shocked sort of way, programmed only to focus on the seemingly endless problems and challenges that inevitably arise when you have a child with LD: doctors, tutors, school meetings; tests, tests and more tests; sleepless hours spent wondering if you're doing the right thing, or if you waited too long, or most harrowing of all, "what's coming next?"

Your other children are doing fine. You're certain of that. You're thankful too. And yes, once in a while they may have to operate on auto-pilot because there's simply no other choice. They need to do it, and more importantly (as far as you're concerned) they *can* do it.

They don't have the same needs as your child with LD.

They don't have the same challenges.

They get good grades and have lots of friends and have social skills appropriate for their age.

They might complain once in a while that you're lavishing too much time and attention on the disabled child, but you understand that sibling rivalry is natural in every family so it's not a big deal. If your non-disabled child develops a serious problem in school or in life, of course you will give him or her as much attention and time as required. You will give *all* your children what they need, when they need it – that is a given – and right now your son or daughter without LD does not seem to need as much as your child with the disability.

That is how most of us view our family dynamic, especially in the years after a diagnosis.

Crisis issues eventually pass and your life as a family settles down, though this does not mean the problems disappear – they don't – but the things that once caused such panic now become routine and most parents have learned enough about the child's disability that it no longer seems as daunting or catastrophic as it once did. And now, just when you thought you could settle into a somewhat normal way of life, along comes the shock of discovering that one of your non-disabled children has been having trouble all along.

This child may have complained about the attention paid to the disabled child. He or she may have cried and asked you repeatedly why you spend so much time with that child instead of with him or her. During the worst of the crisis time, you mentally brushed these concerns aside. You may have listened and assured them that you are doing your best to be fair, but inwardly, you're still so focused on the disabled child that it can be quite difficult to keep what seems to be a small and not-too-serious issue in the forefront of your mind. That's not to say that some can't do it. Some families cope with sibling issues quite well. However, if you went through the trouble of finding this book, I assume your family is not one of these.

You may be a mother at her wit's end, trying as hard as you can to maintain a balance between all of your children, but to no avail. It may be that one or more of your children, with or without LD, have created a toxic atmosphere of hostility and resentment that has a detrimental effect on the entire family. I have seen this happen. The child with the disability causes such havoc through moody behavior or constant demands that everyone else is on edge all the time.

Or maybe the sibling of a child (or adult) with LD lives a life which has become a simmering cauldron of resentment.

Rightly or wrongly, they feel they are The Forgotten Child, overlooked and underappreciated. It is no exaggeration to say that, for some people, the strained relationship with their parents and disabled siblings can cause psychological distress that lasts well into adulthood. I know a young man who simply cannot get past the sense of injustice and wounded anger that has trailed him since childhood, all due to what he perceived as extreme unfairness in the way he was treated versus the way his parents treated his sister with LD. It's easy for us to say, "oh get over it," and I wouldn't be surprised if he didn't say that to himself on occasion, but the human mind is a mysterious thing and for some, "getting over it" is nearly impossible.

I believe that many of the challenges of sibling issues can be narrowed down to the use of one word: *Special.*

We hear it all the time in the disabilities world - special education, special Olympics, special needs — and I have no expectation this will change anytime soon. When we hear it in connection with a person, our minds immediately go to "disability." It has become shorthand for disability. For me, the problem comes when its original meaning becomes entangled in this newer meaning, especially when used around siblings.

Merriam-Webster dictionary defines the word *special* as:

- *different from what is normal or usual;*
- *unusual in a good way :*
- *better or more important than others*
- *especially important or loved*

Regardless of when or how the word is used, we all know this definition. Children know this definition. They may understand the use of the word in connection with education, but can we be sure they understand when they hear a parent use it to describe their brother or sister with LD. There is no question that some will interpret the word as it is traditionally defined: *especially important or loved.* One person we interviewed inspired the subtitle of this book when she told us she heard the word over and over in connection with her disabled sister and could not help but wonder: "If she's so special, what am I?"

This question often resides in the mind and heart of the child who feels overlooked, forgotten, or somehow not as unique or even loved as a brother or sister. There is no point in trying to avoid "special" when used to describe a type of education, or Olympics, or needs; but I wonder if we shouldn't make an effort to choose another word when describing a child with LD.

"He has special needs," means one thing.

"He is special," means quite another.

Most challenges with sibling issues fall somewhere between the two extremes of no problem at all and major problems that cause lasting damage.

Here is a typical example of a family inhabiting that middle ground:

I recently met with a mother named Marianne. We had planned to talk about a school for children with LD in New York, but when I mentioned I was writing this book, she said, "Oh, I could really use a book like that!"

I asked her what she meant.

"I have two children, both daughters," she said. "My eldest, Laura, is now fourteen and does not have LD. My youngest, Ellie, has dyslexia, ADHD – you name it, she has it to one degree or another. When she was first diagnosed, I went through all the panic and confusion that most mothers experience. I realized early on that I was not alone in these feelings. I was lucky to have a friend whose son has LD, so I had a mentor of sorts.

"I got through all the diagnostic tests, I got through all the school meetings, and I even got a handle on the big things such as fears and worries about my daughter's future and if she would ever be able to go to college. I'm OK with all of that. There are still bad days, but overall I think I have a handle on it. The one thing I can't seem to deal with is this whole sibling thing. I must stress that it is not a constant problem. It's not debilitating, the way some of the other problems were. I don't have a house filled with teenage girls screaming at each other or constantly complaining about each other. They are typical teenagers, so I get the occasional sullen attitude or talking back, but nothing unusual.

"The problem is mostly with me. I am aware – I have *always* been aware that there is unequal treatment going on. There is no question that my older daughter Laura does not get the time and attention given to Ellie. She has never said anything to me about it. She is completely understanding and accepting of her sister's disability. That's what she tells me, at least. I truly do believe she understands why I have to spend so much more time with Ellie, but I can't help feeling guilty over it. Often my husband is able to step in, but he's got an incredibly busy work schedule and sometimes events conspire against us. I can't help feeling that Laura may be building up a reserve of resentment that may end up affecting her in some way down the road. It's really a dilemma. It's like you watch yourself doing something you know you need to do, all the while realizing it might be affecting your other child in negative ways."

I asked Marianne if she had an example.

"Yes, I have a very recent example," she said. "A couple of weeks ago, Laura (non-disabled) was going to play in a basketball game. It was a really important game and she had to go away for an overnight trip. She asked if I could be one of the chaperones and come with her and, of course, I said yes. I was so happy because I saw how much it meant to her. She leaped from her chair with a cry of excitement and ran from the room to call one of her friends. Before she was halfway up the stairs, it suddenly hit me. I had already made an appointment the morning after the basketball game to take my younger daughter Ellie for one of her tests. I can't remember which one…there are so many, they all blend together. But I realized if I went along on the overnight trip there was no way I could be back in time, and I couldn't cancel Ellie's appointment as it took over a month to get to see that doctor in the first place."

"What did you do?"

"I sat down at the kitchen table and tried to think it through. I could hear Laura upstairs talking and laughing with her friend. Ellie was in the family room playing a video game. My husband was still at work. I could talk to him about it later, but right then, in that moment, I was at a loss. I didn't know who to talk to or who to call. This kind of problem doesn't seem all that huge in the grand scheme of things. It's hard to get a lot of sympathy or even understanding….no, I take that back. Maybe I would get sympathy and understanding, but I would never have asked for it in the first place. This simply wasn't the kind of problem I would share with anyone except my husband."

"Did you come up with a solution?"

"No. That's the trouble. I never do! I did the same thing I always end up doing. I asked Laura to come downstairs and I broke the news to her. I told her I made a mistake with the dates and that I couldn't go to the game, and that her father would not be able to get the time off from work to take my place. She nodded and said she understood. The truth is, I believe she *did* understand, but that didn't take away her disappointment. It doesn't matter how much she accepted or understood the situation, she was still disappointed. So was I. On top of that, I felt guilty. This sort of thing happens all the time. Laura has to put her life on hold because of her sister's disability. It shouldn't be that way. I try to do everything I can to avoid it. The guilt can become oppressive."

Marianne's situation is far from unique. Many could listen to her story and think that Laura will get over it eventually. After all, it's only a basketball game. And that is true: it *is* only a basketball game. But it's also a school play, a softball game, an outing with friends, a date to buy a dress for the prom; it is a hundred little things that result in a long string of disappointments and expectations to "understand" her sister's disability.

In my experience, it doesn't matter how understanding Laura is: at some point she is bound to feel resentment toward her sister and anger toward her parents. Even the most saintly child is still human. One of the best things Laura has going for her is the fact that her mother realizes this is going on. Acknowledging the problem can truly go a long way toward alleviating it. Some parents raise their children without ever acknowledging the obvious and necessary imbalance of attention and that is when the real trouble begins.

It is not always easy to see this trouble because not all children react to it the same way. Some siblings react with anger and resentment. Some feel an obligation to compensate by becoming the perfect child. Some will try to act as a "third parent" and develop a domineering attitude. Some siblings feel guilty or ashamed of bypassing their brother or sister in certain skills. They run the gamut and trying to figure out which category your children fall into can be a real challenge. Families, too, run the gamut in the ways they handle the challenges. Some parents handle the various dilemmas well. Some are completely done in by the challenge.

Some parents, like the mother who had the meltdown at my speech in Dallas, are consumed with anguish. Others are completely oblivious and do not realize there is any sort of problem at all. These are the mothers who are so confident in their actions and efforts on behalf of their child with a disability that they cannot imagine everyone doesn't fully see things the same way. When it is finally brought to their attention that the non-disabled child has strong feelings of being left out, the mother is floored. She always thought and completely believed she was giving equal attention to all her children.

In this book, we will talk to mothers with varying experiences raising children with and without disabilities. We will also discuss the issue with some adults whose siblings have LD. For some, both parents and their children, the issue is a major one. For others, it is minor and has little effect upon the family. And still others *think* it is a minor issue without ever realizing that it looms large and has damaging effects in the life of their child without LD.

These feelings are a common problem, even in families where there is no disability at all. For example, when one child excels in sports and receives abundant praise, the other one may feel left out. The issues raised in this book can apply to practically any family.

Sibling issues do not always remain confined to difficulties between brothers and sisters. The entire family can be affected. Later in the book we will look at relationships between husbands and wives and how learning disabilities (and sibling issues) have altered, strengthened, or, in some cases, damaged family relationships.

Most of these varying issues will show up within the stories told by mothers and fathers, sisters and brothers; with and without LD.

I begin with my own.

ALESSANDRO AND ALLEGRA:
BROTHER AND SISTER

*H*ere we are on the Long Island Expressway: myself, my son Alessandro and my daughter Allegra, on our way from New York City to Long Island for the weekend.. The traffic is heavy. The outside heat is oppressive. Drivers are honking their horns and cursing. Tempers flare. Everyone wants to get to their destination and escape the madness, and here I am with two children in the back seat arguing over territory.

"You're in my space Allegra!"

"No, I'm not."

"Yes you are — move your foot. Mom, she touched me with her foot!"

I've tried everything. I told them, nicely, to please keep it down as I was trying to concentrate. I then told them, a little less nicely, to knock it off. And now I resort to the big guns. "All right you two. If you don't stop it right now, I'm going to stop this car and let you walk the rest of the way."

"Mom, he keeps making faces at me."

"I am not!"

"He's *looking* at me!"

"Ok, that's it," I tell them. I put on my blinker, inch through the traffic to the side of the road, stop the car and say: "Get out."

Dead silence from the back seat.

"I mean it. Get out."

With a bit more coaxing and a few threats, my two beloved children get out and stand beside the car.

"Good bye," I say. "Have a nice walk."

With that, I inch the car forward about one mile an hour until I can see them in the rear view mirror, walking behind me. I go about ten feet more and then I stop and roll down the window. "OK, you can get in now."

They make no further mention of territorial disputes for the remainder of the trip.

I lead with this charming tale of family togetherness to emphasize that learning disabilities (or disabilities of any kind) should not be, and in all probability, *are* not always the central issue when it comes to sibling difficulties. This is not to minimize their effect, but to point out that they are not the only cause of friction in a family. Beginning with Cain and Abel, siblings throughout history and all around the world have engaged in rivalries and squabbles, and we should not lose sight of this. *Sibling rivalry* is not a term invented due to the presence of a learning disability. It exists wherever there are siblings and whether or not there is a disability involved. That's the way it is with nearly all families, and mine is no different.

My daughter Allegra was born five years after my son Alessandro. Until she was diagnosed with severe learning disabilities, I believed I had two completely typical, well-adjusted children. I was divorced from their father soon after Allegra was born, but both of my children were happy and healthy, and we had a very contented life together in Manhattan with no sign of trouble on the horizon. When Allegra turned five, our lives took a turn that forever altered the course of our future. She began to exhibit what I thought at first was a small behavior problem. She appeared distracted and couldn't sit still. She could not focus. "She'll grow out of it," I thought. By that time she had already gone through two years of preschool and, again, I never heard a word from a teacher or anyone else that anything might be wrong.

Soon after she turned five, when she was in kindergarten, I received a call from Miss Zimmerman, the principal of the school. She asked if I would come in to meet with her to talk about Allegra. I assumed she wanted to talk about her progress or plans for the coming months. At first she sounded positive about how well she was getting on, but she then suggested I have her tested as "she doesn't follow directions, she wanders around the room when she should be sitting down, and most of all, she retreats into a world of her own." None of this was said in an unkindly manner. Miss Zimmerman was trying to be helpful, but the words "you may want to have her tested" sounded alarm bells. I didn't know what she was talking about. Tested for what? She explained further and said, "For learning disabilities," and I stared at her, wondering what on earth that meant. Until that moment, I had never heard of a learning disability, or, if I did, the words went in one ear and out the other.

I sat back in my chair, relieved. Surely, something called learning disabilities wasn't that serious. It must have meant she had a little trouble keeping up with the others. It would all work itself out eventually, wouldn't it?

The meeting with Miss Zimmerman was the first real step on a long, sometimes frustrating, sometimes immensely rewarding journey that continues to this day. Soon after hearing learning disabilities for the first time, my family was thrust headlong into a new, bewildering world of tests, tutors, doctors, schools, rejection, misunderstanding, and most of all (for me), worry and anxiety. Worry and anxiety were my constant companions in those early years (and still show up uninvited from time to time). I had no signposts to follow, no person to confide in, no professional to guide me.

The medical profession was worse than useless. Honestly, they were. If anything, they added fuel to the fire and turned my anxiety into full-blown panic. The first doctor I went to told me she was mentally retarded and should be institutionalized. The second told me there was nothing wrong at all. No one had definitive answers. No one could give me a diagnosis that made sense. There was no Internet back then so I had no access to the wealth of information now available online.

I never knew from one day to the next what would happen or what the doctor might say. Eventually the diagnoses began to fall between the two extremes and after enough doctors came up with that same conclusion, I began to accept the result that she had severe, unspecified, learning disabilities. That is, Allegra has LD to a greater extent than many others, yet they are not so pronounced in any one area that they fall within a specific category. For instance, she has dyslexia as part of her LD, but the term 'Dyslexia' alone cannot possibly cover the full range of her disabilities.

My acceptance of Allegra's diagnosis did not mean an end to the problems.

When I was told she could not be mainstreamed, I researched every LD school in the city and found the one I thought most fitting for her. I brought her in to be interviewed and they told me I could not be in the room with her during the interview. This upset both of us and I am sure affected her responses to their questions. The next day I received a call telling me they would not accept her. The second school did the same. The third did the same. I kept crossing school names off my list until there were none left. Finally, the Gateway School in Manhattan accepted her because someone dropped out and a place became available.

Throughout all this, I allowed her older brother Alessandro to go on auto-pilot for much of his schooling and social life.

And why not? He was fine. He had no disabilities. He had lots of friends. He didn't need the extra attention. He might grumble about it once in a while, but he appeared to get over it soon enough. Surely he understood why I spent so much more time with his sister. It never occurred to me that he might not understand, or might even resent it.

This is not to imply that he was superhuman or a saint – he and Allegra had as normal a brother/sister relationship as is possible. They fought all the time, there were little rivalries and jealousies, and sometimes they drove each other crazy. When there were fights and squabbles, I often did what most mothers do – I threw up my hands and let them battle it out. There was never any real malice involved and never, ever, was the issue of a learning disability used against Allegra. (That's not to say it has never been used *by* Allegra. Once in a while she pulled "But I have a learning disability" out of her hat as an excuse to get out of doing something she didn't want to do. It didn't work.)

The differences in their schooling took its toll as well. Alessandro had homework nearly every night. Allegra, during her early years attending a special school, had no homework at all (though this changed in later years). Rather than make her sit quietly in a corner with nothing to do while Alessandro did his math homework, I allowed her to watch television. So there's Alessandro, struggling over algebra, all the while Allegra is bugging him or singing along to the television at the other end of the room. It didn't take long for this scenario to play itself out exactly as one might expect.

Alessandro: "I don't see why I have to do algebra while she watches The Brady Bunch."

Me: "Because she doesn't have any homework." — an answer I thought both obvious and sufficient.

Alessandro would then utter what should become the official motto of the Organization of Siblings of Children with Disabilities (if there was such a group): "But it's not fair!"

I didn't accept it or understand his feelings. I was tired of hearing this same complaint night after night. I thought *he* was being unreasonable and even a little insensitive and I therefore handled it in one of the worst, most immature ways possible. "Well, maybe you'd like to be her for one day," I shot back. "Maybe *you'd* like to go to all her doctor appointments. Maybe *you'd* like to have no friends."

He would sigh and slap his pencil down on the table and return to his algebra, while Allegra, oblivious to all of this, continued to giggle at the exploits of the Brady's.

As my daughter grew older, my expectations for her academic performance began to diminish while, at the same time, they began to increase for Alessandro. I set the bar higher for him and while I would praise Allegra for bringing home any grade at all, I would frown upon my son's average grades. Eventually his grades began to drop further and he had to hear me scold him for not trying harder.

But at least I was paying attention.

How is that for an insidious remark? Could it be that some children purposely do poorly in school in the hope of gaining some attention from their parents? Yes, it could.

Children with a brother or sister with a learning disability often feel more is expected of them (and often they are right.) For Alessandro, the most difficult thing was his inability to, as he says, "accept the fact that my sister was — and still is — unable to perform certain everyday activities that have become routine to me." When she was unable to read a book or do a simple math problem, he used to ask me over and over again: "But *why* can't she do it?"

He was honestly trying to understand and my response was in keeping with my earlier unhelpful remarks about the television. "Because she can't," I said and left it at that. I completely underestimated his ability to comprehend what was going on. I am quite sure he would have understood Allegra and her disability a lot better if I had taken the time to explain things to him as they were happening. In my defense, I will say that one of the reasons I didn't explain was because, at that time, I still didn't know what was going on. As Alessandro said, "I think in a strange way, I sort of lived through the discovery of Allegra's LD along with my mother, though I think I came at it from a much more ignorant place and didn't really understand what was happening. I saw my mother's frustration and the questions that were coming up such as 'Why isn't this happening yet?' or 'Why isn't she able to do that yet?' but none of us fully realized what all these questions would eventually lead to."

He is absolutely right: I had no firm idea of what was going on – or if anything serious was going on at all. We were still careening from diagnosis to diagnosis and I found the prospect of explaining all that to a twelve year old close to impossible. Regardless, I feel I should have made the effort to try for I now know how important it is to include the sibling in every step along the way.

Many years later Alessandro made the same point in a speech he gave at the annual fundraising benefit for the National Center for Learning Disabilities. This is what he said:

"My mother is Chairman of the National Center for Learning Disabilities, or NCLD. Sometimes I imagine myself as Chairman of the NCSPLDWDNNHLDT, or National Center for Siblings of People with Learning Disabilities Who Do Not Necessarily Have LD Themselves. Our mission would be to teach parents and teachers of children with LD how to cope with their children who do not have learning disabilities. In reaction to the limitations faced by their children with LD, parents should be wary of expecting too much from their children who do not have LD. I always felt that because Allegra could not perform as a regular student, the weight of scholastic achievement rested on my shoulders. It is extremely important to educate siblings as to exactly what their brothers or sisters are experiencing. It was very hard for me to understand why Allegra could learn to become an expert figure skater but met with constant frustration with her reading, writing or math skills. I saw my mother's heart sink and Allegra's teachers become resigned to their lack of success in helping her to learn. I did not buy that for one minute. But then again, I did not know what a lot of parents and teachers know. So while I was punished for getting bad grades, I saw Allegra getting comforted. While I was pushed to do better, Allegra was allowed to move on and sidestep the problems arising from her education. To all parents, I cannot stress enough how important it is to allow your other children to share in what you are learning about LD. If I knew then what I know now, everything would have been a lot clearer."

Alessandro once told me that he envied Allegra at times for having a "defined diagnosis." A failing grade for her was expected and accepted. For him, a failing grade meant personal failure. Long after leaving school, he went to an ophthalmologist, and while in the waiting room, he noticed a pamphlet that linked difficulties in school with vision problems. "A-ha!" he thought, "that's my problem!" But he quickly realized that was not the case as he had no problem with his vision while back in school.

Another issue that often comes up when comparing the experiences of siblings, disabled and not, involves friendships and social skills. These can be truly gut-wrenching and, for me, caused some of my deepest sadness and greatest angst. Often the siblings are peripheral to the actual problem. In our case, for instance, Alessandro had a multitude of friends while Allegra struggled to keep even one friendship intact. But that wasn't Alessandro's fault. He was fun and witty and popular with his classmates. Most who knew him, loved him. Allegra was fun and witty too, in her own way, but her peers didn't quite understand her, they couldn't connect, and some were bewildered by the effects of her learning disabilities. We spent our summers in Long Island and no one in our circle of friends had a child with any sort of disability at all, and truthfully, their parents were not willing to try to understand how difficult things were for Allegra — and things *were* difficult. An example would be games: Allegra had a great deal of trouble understanding the rules of almost any game, and though she wanted to play and was an enthusiastic player, she sometimes didn't follow the proper rules. The other children couldn't understand why, especially if they were younger. I vividly recall Allegra playing a board game with some children who were quite a bit younger than she was at the time. She wasn't able to follow the instructions and this led to accusations of cheating by the two younger ones — a thing Allegra would never do on purpose. They simply could not comprehend that a "big girl" couldn't understand the rules they knew so well.

Invitations to cookouts and parties came all the time — for Alessandro. The phone rang day and night — for Alessandro. Kids came over to our house all the time for overnights — with Alessandro.

Allegra, meanwhile, would answer the phone every time it rang, hoping one of her "friends" would be on the other end, but that never happened. Sometimes she took matters into her own hands and would make the call herself. I would cringe when I heard her in the other room asking if one of the neighborhood girls could come over to play followed by the inevitable disappointment.

Sometimes I tried to ease this situation by asking Alessandro to bring his sister with him when he was heading out to play, and this had predictable results. He was horrified, and I must stress that this had nothing to do with her having LD: it had everything to do with a twelve year old boy being asked to bring his seven year old sister along to play with his friends. He rebelled, I insisted, he rebelled again, I backed down. Sometimes he agreed, and I'm sure Allegra had a fine time though I'm equally sure Alessandro was as miserable as any other boy would be in that situation.

The truth of this is that I cannot say with certainty that Allegra was as affected by her lack of friends as I was. It tore at my heart. It really did. If you ask Allegra now about those years, she will tell you with great sincerity that she had "tons of friends." An LD professional once told me that Allegra has mirrored Alessandro's experiences. She knows that Alessandro had friends and she truly believes she did too. If this is what she believes, I am not going to say otherwise or try to correct her. I cannot forget those lonely days. If she can, or if she has transformed them, then I say good for her.

When asked if he was ever embarrassed by Allegra in those days, Alessandro says "I don't think embarrassed would be the word for it, though I think there were times when I was probably rolling my eyes. It was not so much when we were home but on a trip somewhere. I can't say it was because of her disability but it could very well have been that she was my little sister and I really didn't want to be burdened with her. Having said that, there were times when Allegra would open her mouth and I could tell something was going to come out that was probably not the right thing to say. But what I found was that when this happened, it affected me so much more than anyone else in the room. I remember once, I was probably in my 30s, and we went to see Gregory Hines on Broadway. We got to go backstage and meet him. Allegra honed in on a movie he had been in called *White Nights*. She was like, 'You're the guy who was in that movie,' and I was thinking, 'Oh Allegra, please don't.' But he was charmed by it. It was some random movie that he'd done and not many people remembered it. He thought it was so nice of her to remember. Allegra does that a lot. She picks up on things that others don't, and she will say it out loud where you or I think 'I could never say that.' I am happy to say that for the most part my friends loved Allegra and she loved them. She was kind to them and to the best of my knowledge, they were kind to her."

I always knew Alessandro would be out on his own after leaving college, but especially in the early years, I assumed Allegra and I would spend our lives together. Like many parents of children with severe LD, I never imaged she would be able to live on her own. This may have been her fate had she not found a passion in her life: figure skating. It became her great joy. She started when she was young and continued on in her teen years. In order to improve (something she was determined to do), she was required to move to Lake Placid up in the Adirondack Mountains of New York where she lived with her coach. This was her first time away from home and she thrived there. At fifteen she went to boarding school for students with special needs on Cape Cod. This was a very difficult period for both of us as I would have given anything to keep her with me but no school in New York would take her – even the schools specifically for children with learning disabilities. I never understood their decisions then, and still don't – Allegra never had emotional problems, was never disruptive, and was never dismissed from any school she ever attended. Her grades were no worse than other students with LD, and may have been better. It remains a mystery to me that every school she ever attended took her on a conditional basis, warning me that if she couldn't keep up in the first year, she would have to leave…and that never happened, not once. She always kept up and surpassed expectations.

During these later school years, Alessandro and Allegra did not spend much time together. This would be the same in any family, I'm sure, when one is off to college and the other is still in the early years in high school. We spent holidays together, of course, and part of the summer, but I knew the time would soon come when Alessandro would be graduating from college and off living on his own and I decided we should take one last vacation together as a family. I thought it would be a wonderful idea to go to Austria around Christmas to hear a concert by the Vienna Boys' Choir and go on a *Sound of Music* Tour (the movie is still a favorite of mine and Allegra's). We had not traveled together for years and trouble started when we reached London and Allegra turned to me and announced, "I want to go home."

I thought maybe she was suffering from jet-lag and didn't pay too much attention, but things got a lot worse when we finally arrived in Vienna. She seemed determined to not enjoy herself. She would cry for no reason. We went to a concert featuring Placido Domingo, and there she sat, between me and Alessandro, with her arms crossed and a frown on her face, paying no attention to the music. I looked over her at Alessandro with a frustrated expression that asked, 'What are we going to do?'

Things did not improve the next day or the next, but rather, my mood darkened into growing anger. I could not understand this willful determination to remain as miserable and stubborn as possible. Nothing seemed to penetrate her guarded shell — music, restaurants, sight-seeing; everything passed by without effect and causing no glimmer of joy or even a smile. Never in her (then) sixteen years had I ever seen that side of her.

I was disappointed. I had hoped to have a happy family vacation and it was falling apart. "Maybe we should go home," I said but Alessandro would not give in.

"Let me talk to her," he said, and he took her aside for a heart-to-heart. Allegra immediately began to cry and Alessandro immediately understood something I did not: she missed home but it was more than that. She was frightened. She didn't understand the language. Signs were written in German. She didn't understand the money. Nothing was familiar. Nothing reminded her of home. Allegra, like many individuals with LD, is a person of strict routine and habit. Change comes slowly and with great difficulty. With best intentions, I had taken her out of her structured world and brought her into one filled with confusing, unfamiliar things. For once she was out of her "box" and it was not working.

Alessandro pulled her back from that place. He took her aside and talked to her, he made her smile and then laugh (he did this by quoting lines from her favorite comedies — always a surefire way to get Allegra to laugh), and with his help, she eased herself into the experience of Vienna. When we visited Salzburg we took the *Sound of Music* tour and when it was over she turned to me and said, "Mom, that was the best trip ever!"

It truly was, and it was entirely due to Alessandro's understanding and patience.

Years have passed since then. Both Alessandro and Allegra live on opposite sides of the country. They don't see each other often, though they have agreed to have a weekly phone conversation every Tuesday night to talk about the ups and downs of their lives. Learning disabilities no longer play a role in their relationship as brother and sister — or rather, they no longer play a predominant role. Both of my children have settled into lives that best suit them, and this has worked out well for their relationship. Unlike the early years, Allegra truly does have many friends who love her and watch over her.

After many years in Lake Placid, she moved to Cambridge, MA to start a new, independent life, but the challenges have not come to an end. Every parent of a child with LD knows that sooner or later the disability will appear again in some way to cause a problem, a situation, sometimes a crisis — depending on the day. Even so, the severity of these challenges has diminished considerably.

Alessandro (thankfully) appears not to be burdened with the lingering resentments felt so often by people who have siblings with disabilities. "If there is any resentment over this whole sibling issue," he says, "I think it came about because my mother was so overly-concerned that I would reject Allegra or push her away. She really made an effort to push us together and sometimes it was a bit much. It even happened after I was married. I remember a Christmas when the whole family was together and my wife and I had just been married for a short time. We had made New Year's plans and my mother said, 'You have to include your sister.' I was like, 'Really? You're still doing that?' This was going to be my first New Year's Eve with my wife and I was supposed to include my sister? I don't think Allegra would have cared either way. I think it's still a struggle for my mother to decide how much to be a part of Allegra's life, and when to step in and when to step out. It's always difficult, especially when the child is an adult and living on her own. I don't envy my mother that dilemma because I think it is a genuine dilemma. It's all about when to stop being the nurturing mother and when to let Allegra fend for herself. And that is the heart of one of my life-long debates with my mother. Where does Allegra's limitation really cut her off? I always felt that she was capable of doing more than Mom was allowing her to do. Beyond all the issues related to Allegra's disability, there was a very traditional brother/sister relationship that existed between us. We fought like any other siblings and I think that was healthy for both of us. I never really treated Allegra any differently. I gave her a really hard time. She gave me a really hard time. We never beat each other up or anything like that, but she really would aggravate the hell out of me sometimes and I know I did the same to her."

When asked if Alessandro ever has any fears for Allegra's future he answers with an emphatic — "No, I don't. She lives in a different city on the other side of the country from me and she is living an independent life. Like all of us, she's susceptible to anything. Something could go wrong. But we can say that about anyone. Something could go wrong with any one of us and there's nothing our parents can do about it anymore. Allegra's in the same situation. She may be a little bit more vulnerable than most, but beyond whatever else you want to say, I believe the fact that she has been able to live an independent happy life is Allegra's — and my mother's — greatest accomplishment."

"Love is Not Time"
The Challenges of LD and Siblings

*L*earning disabilities are as varied as the individual children who have them. The same goes for families. Each one, with varying family dynamics, ages, personalities has a unique story. Even so, when the family dynamics involve a child with LD, common threads are woven through each story. They are the challenges we all experience to one extent or another. The details may change, but the stories offer a broad range of experiences — some you may relate to, some you may view as cautionary tales, and some will give you tips on how you may improve your own situation. I met with mothers over the course of several months to talk about sibling issues as they relate to their school-aged children. One group of mothers came from The Gateway School in New York City. A second group came from the Craig School, a school for children with LD and related disorders in Mountain Lakes, New Jersey. In addition, I spoke to a mother of young twins in Texas, one with special needs and one without. Moving from school-age children to teenagers, I spoke with a mother about her two sons and how their high school and early college years were affected by LD.

I did not go into these discussions with any expectations. I simply asked them to talk about their experiences raising a family with both disabled and non-disabled children in the hope of learning what worked and what didn't.

Here are their variations on the same theme:

THE GATEWAY SCHOOL

"What is the greatest challenge for parents when it comes to sibling issues?" I asked Dr. Robert Cunningham, headmaster of the Gateway School in Manhattan.

"There are a few," he said. "I think equity and fairness is something that parents are always struggling with, so the question becomes how to address the fact that they need to spend more time with one child or that the needs of that one child tend to dictate what the family does. They want to know how to make sure the child with a disability feels like an equal part in the family and that the parents are attuned to his or her needs. Parents feel guilty about that, and it comes up in almost every parent/teacher conference. It almost always comes up around the issue of fairness and how to help the child without the disability understand."

"How do you answer those concerns?"

"Let's use homework as an example. In this case you would say to the child without LD, 'there is a right amount of homework for your brother to do, and there is a right of homework for you to do.' It is perfectly fine to help them understand that as a parent, you're meeting the needs of all your children. We've even invited siblings here to see the differences in the school, especially older siblings. The other issue that comes up during conferences is how involved the parent should be in trying to explain things to the brother or sister without LD. One of the things we do at Gateway is to equip the child with LD to deal with peers and to explain and to advocate for themselves, but when they try to do that with their brother or sister, the parent jumps in. The parent then says to me 'I wish I could just stop myself from doing that.'"

"What do you say?"

"I say, 'Yeah, you're right – you should stop yourself from doing that.' And that is part of what we do. We work with children on self-advocacy and we work with them on awareness and understanding of their own disabilities, so when they're equipped for that and they're ready to do it, the parents have to let them do it. "

"Why do so many parents find that so difficult?"

"We always talk about how hard the child works. But the parents work too. They put in so much time, so much emotion and so much energy into trying to make things better for this child, that sometimes when things *are* better for the child, those parents don't recognize it. Rationally, they understand that the kid can do things, but emotionally they're not quite ready for that."

"So even in this issue it's a matter of letting go."

"Sometimes, yes."

"Like saying, 'OK, there's nothing more I can do,' even though you never really feel that way," I said. "You always think there's just one more step, or if I just do one more thing..."

I don't remember anyone suggesting I bring Alessandro to the Gateway school so he could see where his sister was going to school, but I do remember that I did bring him there, and I remember the bewildered, terrified look on his face when he walked through the door. At that time, Gateway was much different than the gleaming, structured school of today. It was in a converted gym, surrounded by tiny makeshift cubicles used as classrooms. There were far fewer students then, and they had far more obvious disabilities. I understood Alessandro's reaction perfectly as I had a similar reaction on my first visit.

Allegra's kindergarten was in the same building as the original Gateway School. When her headmistress suggested I have her tested for 'learning problems,' she also suggested I visit the school on an upper floor as she thought it would be perfect for my daughter. I had not even had Allegra tested at that time, was unclear as to what learning problems she had, and I was therefore shocked when I visited the school. I couldn't believe someone would think she belonged there. But first impressions do not last. Allegra did end up going to the Gateway School for five years and I will remain forever grateful to them for setting her on the right path. It was exactly the right school at the right time, though I couldn't know that at the time. Alessandro didn't know what to make of it either. He struggled to understand why his sister was in a school of children with such obvious disabilities, but I still feel it was important to let him see for himself (though, obviously, I should have followed this up with a heart-to-heart talk and provided answers to all his questions).

I have visited the Gateway School several times in recent years and much has changed. It is a much larger school now and one of the finest in the city. I asked Dr. Cunningham if he could arrange a meeting with some of the mothers of current students to discuss some of the difficulties and challenges they experience with sibling issues.

We met in a vacant room off the library, with three mothers on one side of a long table and me on the other. They were Valerie, who has a daughter named Olivia, born with severe LD. Beside her sat Rosemary, also with a daughter with LD named Samantha, with the nickname "Sam." Sam's diagnoses include ADHD-combined type (she is both hyper and inattentive), LD-NOS, Anxiety Disorder-NOS, and Dysgraphia. (NOS, Not Otherwise Specified, means she doesn't specifically fit the classic definitions of these conditions. The Board of Education gives her the disability classification of OHI, Other Heath Impairment. Dysgraphia is a learning disability that affects writing, which requires a complex set of motor and information processing skills.)

Last was Suzanne, whose son Gregory suffers from severe ADHD.

I began with Valerie and asked her to give an overview of her experiences with sibling issues. She didn't hesitate but went directly to the heart of the problem. "I have three children, two daughters and a son," she said. "My son Ryan is the eldest at fifteen. My oldest daughter is Jenny, age fourteen. My youngest is a daughter named Olivia. She is ten and she has LD. My other daughter Jenny does not have disabilities. She is four years older than Olivia, and she is mean."

"Jenny is mean to Olivia?" I asked.

"Yes. I think it's partly a sister thing. But at the same time, Olivia stands too close when she talks. She asks too many questions. She's annoying. And

Jenny, instead of infantilizing Olivia and treating her like a child with disabilities, will say; 'Get out of my room, don't touch my things, and don't ever come in here again. You are the most annoying person.' She says really mean things, though she never goes to the bad place and says truly hateful things."

I asked if Jenny ever invites friends over to visit or if she found Olivia's behavior too embarrassing for that.

"Yes, she has friends over sometimes," Valerie said, "but there was a period when she didn't extend too many invitations because Olivia gets right in the thick of it and wants to join in. She was an embarrassment for Jenny. Recently, for the first time in a long time Olivia was with Jenny and some of her friends – but it was a surprise party for Jenny, so I can't really say she knew beforehand that Olivia would be there. Jenny was over the moon happy with the party, but even so, my heart stood still because I could see her tense up a little bit as Olivia walked around the table to say hello to everybody."

"Was there a problem?" I asked.

"Not at all. We've known all these girls for years. Each of them knows about Olivia and they all got up and posed with her for a picture."

"So it didn't bother anyone?"

"Nobody flinched," Valerie said. "And Olivia was so excited to have all these pictures. I thought to myself, 'See? They're all fourteen. This is not hard for them. They're mature enough that it's not embarrassing for them.' They've known Olivia since they were very young. It's not like she's going to a sleep-over with them. Now, if it had not been a surprise party and if I had said to Jenny beforehand, 'We're going to have a dinner party for you, and Olivia will be there and hang around the whole time,' she would have had a problem with it."

"Did Jenny ever ask you what's wrong with Olivia?"

"When she was younger, yes. We all had difficulty understanding what was wrong. The diagnosis sort of unfolded over time. And I have to tell you... Olivia is ten and half years old and there is still a question of what, exactly, the problem is. She has a really serious vision problem. Essentially, she is legally blind. We knew she had trouble seeing, but she compensates the hell out of everything so it was very hard to tell. I wouldn't put her behind the wheel of a car, but she totally manages with most other things. Even so, if you were talking to her, you would notice something. She stands next to you rather than in front because she sees better peripherally. That's how you can tell she has a vision disability. But it took a really long time to identify how bad her vision was. That was this year's news flash: her vision is very bad. So I would say that to my older kids, 'Olivia really can't see you very well. That is why she goes up against the TV with her nose.' It's the most annoying thing for them because she stands there like a Garfield cat in front of the television all the time – and that's annoying! So she gets yelled at. When the older kids wanted to watch *American Idol*, we're all in the room watching the show and there's Olivia moving back and forth in front of the big screen. She wants to see it all. I'll ask her to sit down and she'll listen and sit for a few minutes and then she crawls back up again."

"She does it because she can't see."

"Right. But earlier, nobody knew how bad her vision was because all these years it wasn't that big a deal. She didn't block the TV when she was younger. But now she's asserting herself and saying, 'This is how I can see.' So now we can bring that to the table with the other kids and say she really can't see the TV unless her nose is on the screen.

"Maybe you should get another TV," I suggested.

"We did. We got a big fat one for her because she enjoys television, even though she has no one to watch TV with because she's annoying. So that sort of diffused that problem. Her other issue is that she doesn't speak very well or clearly. So the others will ask why it's so hard to understand her. I'll tell them I don't exactly know why and I sort of parse it out with them. We never had the blessing of a firm diagnosis. I could never say 'this is what she has and this is what we're doing.' She's a complicated kid."

"What kind of diagnosis did you get?" I asked.

"Nothing definitive. We never got a firm answer. They called it a 'Constellation of Disabilities'. She's got a lot of things. One of the doctors called it 'Otherwise health-impaired,' whatever that means. She was never diagnosed as having a learning disability, mostly because she was reading at grade level."

"She was able to keep up with the class?"

"Yes," Valerie said, "but with her face down on the book. She sort of made it work for as long as she could. At home that presented a complicated profile for her siblings. She could do some things great, but other things like tying her shoes and combing her hair and brushing her teeth were a challenge. So I would explain to my daughter and son (who are both older than Olivia), 'some things are hard for her. Her hands don't work so well.' I tried to keep it simple for them."

"I don't understand why the school didn't ask you to get an outside diagnosis," I said.

"We've been going to doctors forever," Valerie said. "She's got the vision problems and she's got cleft palate, so there are some things we can identify. But even that has presented problems. Her vision, for example. When I asked how bad it was, they said, 'We can see what's wrong with her eyes but we don't know what she sees.' So it's been gradually unfolding bit by bit."

"If you had a more firm diagnosis, you would have had something to tell her sister," I said. "It would have been easier to get a handle on it."

"Yes, that's right. My daughter Jenny, who is now fourteen, would ask me at different times, 'Does she have autism?' She knew about autism. Our friend's child has autism. Olivia in no way has the same profile as that child, but they're somewhat similar as far as their needs. They were two different types of disabilities, but at the same time, I can understand why Jenny would ask. She wanted an answer."

"And autism is talked about so much that children hear about it and know about it."

"Right," Valerie said. "Other possible things might pop into her head, but autism was the only thing she could connect it to, even though she could see Olivia was different than the boy we know with autism. That boy doesn't speak. Olivia never stops talking. So there are different things. But I wish I could have said something definitive when Jenny asked. I wish I could have been able to say, 'Olivia has this long list of things and here is why and here is what we're going to do and here's how we expect it to unfold'. I have never received a roadmap from any doctor. All they ever say is, 'We'll see how it goes.' When Olivia started kindergarten, I heard, 'we'll see how she can manage…we'll see.'"

"I have talked to some adults who had siblings with LD," I said. "They felt like nothing was good enough while they were growing up. They felt they could never do enough to get the same kind of attention as the child with LD. Did you have any experience with that?"

"Olivia is my youngest child, so that gives me a little bit of coverage in terms of giving her more," Valerie said. "She is the baby and they're older. My son is great with Olivia. There's no competition. He loves her. He is supportive of her. He is kind. He sometimes roughs her up in a way that is helpful. They have a great relationship, and I think temperamentally, they're fine. He's old enough and sturdy enough and secure enough. He never says, 'how come you didn't come to my baseball game?' Whenever he would ask me to go, I would say, 'Olivia can't go, and so I can't go. Daddy and I decided that would be too cruel to leave her home with a babysitter while the rest of us go to your baseball game every Saturday.' So that was that. He never made a big deal of it. My daughter, on the other hand, is ruthless about how unfair everything is, and how unfair I am. You know how kids do that? It's not, 'remember the time you didn't come to my school event?' – it's 'you *never* come to my school events.' And that's not true. But to her, anytime I don't make an event, I've missed them all. She counts everything and will say, 'Oh, you're taking Olivia to the movies. When I wanted to go the movies, we never went to the movies.' That makes me feel like being the mean mother back to her. I'll say, 'You know what? You can go to the movies with your friends. If I don't take Olivia to the movies and if I don't take her ice skating, it's not happening for her. You're older.' I say that sort of thing. I know it is like Bad Parenting 101, but I can't help but think she doesn't have the same troubles that Olivia has and that it's unfair to hold me to the same standard. She is able to do pretty much anything she wants on her own. She doesn't need me to get up and go, but if I don't really dig deep and create activities for Olivia, she's going to be home alone and that's not good for her and its not good for me. So I'll say, 'Yes, we are going to the American Girl store. And no, we're not going to Abercrombie for you. You're welcome to come to the American Girl store with us because that's the activity for now.' But she really tries to keep it even-steven. Like, 'why can't we go to Abercrombie, that's where I want to go, and you *never* want to go where I want to go.' It's 'never' or 'always' with her. She's relentless. And as she's gotten older she digs her heels in even more. She's not mean to her sister about the fairness issue. She's mean to her about sibling stuff, like 'you ate all the strawberries, you always get to eat all the strawberries, I never get to eat the strawberries.' But she's mean to me about the division of attention, and that's not a fair fight. So try as I might to explain to her that the needs are greater for Olivia, she doesn't go with it."

I asked the group if any of their other children ever complained about how much time they spend with the child with LD, and they all whole-heartedly agreed that they heard such complaints all the time.

"You're constantly explaining it," Rosemary said. "You're constantly try-ing to improvise and make up for lost time. I try to do volunteer work at both schools and pick up my child two to three days at Gateway and two to three days at my others kids' school – but I always end up doing more here at

Gateway. I have three children. My eldest daughter Samantha is thirteen and has special needs. My son Tony is eleven and my youngest daughter is eight."

I asked Rosemary if she had ever tried to talk to her other children about Samantha's disabilities.

"In general terms, yes. We say it's very hard for Samantha to stop talking, or I'll say something like, 'You know how you feel when you're really angry? When a little thing happens to Samantha, it feels like you do when you're most angry, so that's why she yells.' I try to explain it that way. Here at Gateway, the students go through a 'Myself as a Learner' class. So we then had to start using the right terms for the disability. Before that, we had always used simple terms."

"What do you mean by simple terms? Do you have an example?"

"We spoke in general about what was challenging for Sam — instead of saying she had ADHD we would say it was difficult for her to pay attention, or instead of using the word dysgraphia, we would say it's harder for her to write or draw because her muscles work differently. When Samantha switched schools, we had to spin that as well. We talked about finding a school that fits Sam. I would say finding a school is like finding a shoe that fits. If you have the wrong shoe you get a blister and you can't run, so the new school fits like the right shoe. We built up Gateway like that. But then my other two kids would ask for confirmation that their school is still a good fit for them. We had to reassure them. Another example is that I took the kids to see the musical *Rain* and Samantha started crying. She has some sensory issues as well and the sound and the lights were too much for her. The other kids were whooping it up and there was a group of twelve-year olds having a birthday party behind us, and there was Samantha snuggled up to me, burying her face. The kids in our group asked what happened to Sam and I explained that she is really good at sensing everything—that's why she is so good at knowing what is going on with people and what they are feeling, so when something is that loud and has that much light, it overloads her. And my son said, "What do I have that makes me good?" We had emphasized Sam's challenges as gifts so much that the other kids felt left out. Of course, we took the time to remind the siblings that they were wonderful in their own ways as well. As for Samantha herself, I tell her, 'When you're ready, we'll tell your younger brother about ADHD.' Well, of course one day, Sam is arguing with her brother and she impulsively blurts out, 'Tony made fun of my disability! He was making fun of me because I have ADHD!' Tony was confused and said, 'Mom, what's ADHD?' So that became the springboard for that conversation and it was actually helpful. We could define ADHD as all those simple terms we had used earlier—it makes it hard to pay attention, it makes her more impulsive, more emotional, etc. Our pediatrician has also been really helpful with this. At my son's last check up, he asked how he was getting along with Samantha. He reminded Tony that he needs a little more patience with her. That was nice for him to hear from someone else."

"Does your child with LD use the disability to get away with things?" I asked.

"Not very often," Rosemary said. "That was the first time. And of course, we didn't buy her story at all. I knew her brother didn't know the term ADHD. Occasionally she says, 'I can't do it because of my disability.' When she says that, she's usually on the mark about it. She'll say 'there's just too much stuff going on! I can't do all this!' and she's usually right."

"Do you let her get away with more than the others?"

"I try to keep things balanced, but it gets hard," Rosemary said. "She has less play-dates because it's so hard to coordinate with other LD kids, and she has less homework than the others. I tend to count on her younger siblings for things like helping around the house because they are more reliable and less dramatic about it. I guess part of the problem is her immaturity too: I can give my younger daughter a bigger strawberry and that can cause a meltdown.

"Figuring out the balance of attention seems to be the eternal problem," I said. "I think it can be as hard for the mother as it for the children."

Suzanne now joined in the conversation. She raised her hand and said, "I missed my daughter's birthday just last week because I was at group therapy with my son Gregory. I have three children, Gregory who is thirteen, Elliot who is ten and a daughter Andrea who is eight. Gregory, my eldest, has severe ADHD and he is the oldest so it's really difficult for me. I'm watching my younger eight-year-old child have to suck up and be the older one. It's terrible. And luckily I have an amazing baby-sitter who is probably more loved than I am by my eight-year-old daughter."

"Oh, no, don't say that," I said, seeing that Suzanne was about to cry.

"It's true," she said and the tears began to flow. "The baby-sitter was the one who was there to create a special birthday dinner for her. I totally think she spends more quality time with my eight year old than I do and that just kills me. It kills me."

"But what can you do?" I asked. "There's only so much you can do about it."

"That's true," Rosemary said. "You run around like a maniac. It's like, OK, I'm going to bring my son to his sports practice and I can be there for 15 minutes before I have to take Samantha to an appointment. I'm there at his practice for a few minutes and hope that it counts."

"Does it count?"

"Sometimes he'll ask why I can't stay and I'll say I'm going to Samantha's psychiatrist. If he says something about it, I'll say, 'aren't you lucky you're not going to the psychiatrist?'"

Suzanne said, "When I look at the photographs of my other children's life, it seems the baby-sitter took them all. It's terrible."

"Does she know you feel so badly about it?" I asked.

"Yes, she knows. My house is pretty open about what is wrong with everybody. My brother-in-law wrote a book about depression. My son Gregory was diagnosed with an anxiety disorder along with ADHD so my whole entire family understands everything."

"What did you say to Gregory?" I asked.

"He started taking medication four years ago. At the time I said, 'Gregory, I also take medication to help with my brain chemistry,' so it wouldn't seem like such an unusual thing to do."

"Does he feel better when he's on the medication?"

"Yes, much better. He's really fine now. But I also have a problem with my younger son. He feels a sense of loss over Gregory's disability. He really looked up to Gregory. Gregory was his idol and his best friend, and now it's changed. Gregory doesn't talk to him anymore. He's unpredictable. He's angry."

"So your younger son feels he lost his best friend," I said.

"Yes. It's terrible. It's hard for me to watch it. Last summer, Gregory said, 'No one wants to play with me.' But the thing is, he's not trustworthy. You never know how he'll react. You don't know if he's going to turn on you. You don't know what's going to happen. It's difficult for other children. His temper is so unregulated and he's so unpredictable."

"I went through something similar with my children diverging in their abilities," Rosemary said. "For me, last year was the year that my fourth grader's work went beyond my sixth grader's work. In my younger son's class, the writing had to be in cursive. Samantha's Occupational Therapy goal is to be able to sign her last name. I can remember her walking past his homework and looking at it and saying, 'He did this?' And my seven year old is meticulous about her writing and her drawing. She'll write her thank you letters beautifully. Samantha, who is older, will write a note with a little stick figure and it looks like kindergarten work."

"But it's okay," I said.

"It's okay, yes," Rosemary agreed. "It's all okay."

THE CRAIG SCHOOL

*M*ountain Lakes, N.J. is a beautiful little lakeside town about an hour outside of New York City. I had given a talk at a school for children with LD called The Craig School, and asked if I could come back to talk to some of the mothers about sibling issues. They enthusiastically agreed and we met in what they call the Blue House, once a residence but now converted into offices, where I sat at a table with four women, Nancy, Kathy, Sally and Marla. These are their stories, told in their own words.

NANCY
"Fair isn't Equal"

Nancy began by saying, "I have one child with LD who has six siblings. I have seven children. And I should clarify – Meg, my 'most LD child,' has three siblings who are also affected by some degree of language-based learning disability, though all are milder than Meg's. Meg has LD and ADHD. She didn't have any extreme behavior problems, but she certainly had some minor and annoying behaviors that impacted the family. In our case, what could have been more pronounced problems with her behavior became dissipated because there were so many people around who would tell her, 'Oh, get over it.' They wouldn't tolerate her 'Debbie Downer' behavior, so that may have helped her come down to a normal level. I must say though, I was always perplexed by the fact that Meg's sisters would not be more sympathetic as they also had some learning issues. They didn't cut her much slack at all. Meg saw herself as 'much less smart' than her sisters and always felt like the 'different one' in the family. I think her more mildly LD-affected sisters looked at Meg with impatience and disdain. They thought she was ridiculous in her behavior and didn't show much tolerance. At the same time, the more siblings there are, the more it may help the child with LD gain some perspective. They see how others handle issues, and they also can't get away with things they might if they were an only child or only one of two children. I've often been so thankful that Meg has such a big family. I think if I had only had just her, it would have been much more difficult."

"That's probably true," I said. "She has been exposed to a lot of people who know how to deal with her."

"Exactly," Nancy said. "If she had only had one sibling, it probably would have been very difficult because I would constantly be trying to find the balance between the two."

"How do the others relate to Meg?"

"At one time or another they have all criticized me and said things like 'Oh, Mom, you treat Meg differently,' or 'how come she isn't held to the same standards? Her room is a total wreck and you never make her clean it up.'"

"What did you say to them?"

"I said, 'You're right! I finally gave up trying to make her do it!' But in general, I'll say something like 'Fair isn't Equal.'"

"What do you mean by that?"

"I mean that every child is different and they all need to be treated differently. Meg has different needs than the others."

"Do they accept that?"

"I think so. Through the years of living with her, they all understand how frustrating and difficult some of her behaviors can be, and how difficult it is to figure out what to do about it. I still have trouble with that. I have even solicited advice from my other children and asked them, 'How would *you* handle this? What do you think we should do?' They would give me sympathetic shrugs of their shoulders and say they didn't know."

"Is there any animosity between the siblings?" I asked.

"There is some, yes," Nancy said. "They all get annoyed by some of her behavior, just as I do. She will take things from one of her sister's room, for example. That might be fine in a young child but she's nineteen and she is *still* doing it. Andrea, her next youngest sister, was on Facebook the other night and saw a picture of Meg wearing a dress Andrea had bought over the summer. Meg had taken it to college with her. That's an example of her annoying behavior. I feel she should have outgrown that sort of thing. I always think we should be beyond this, but we're not. Meg has never responded to discipline in a normal manner. She didn't seem to learn from her mistakes. This has been going on in my house for years. Things would disappear, they would reappear, they'd be under the bed, or in a shoe or a boot – 'Oh, you weren't hiding it?' I'd say. 'Then why is it in your boot?'"

"Did you ever explain to the others what was going on with Meg?"

"Yes. I would say things like, 'Meg has more trouble learning.' They knew that because she was pulled out for special education in elementary school. She was always in a different school than theirs. We used to live in Buffalo, NY. My husband got a job in New Jersey. We had planned to keep the family in Buffalo and he would commute. But at that point, Meg was about to go into middle school and there were no good schools for children with LD close to us in Buffalo. I basically moved my entire family on behalf of Meg. I wanted to get more school options for her. I knew my other children would adjust, especially the younger ones. Once we moved, it was difficult. My two oldest were finishing high school back in Buffalo and the rest were here in New Jersey, Meg in the LD private school and the other ones in public school. I was going back and forth between Buffalo, NY and Mountain Lakes, NJ. It was crazy for a couple of years."

I pointed out that this was a perfect example of parents who have every intention of being equal and fair, though in reality, there is always the one child who needs more.

"Right!" Nancy said. "But what other choice do you have? You have to do all you can to give that child as solid a chance in the world as possible."

KATHY
"Accepting the 'No'"

"I have a little different situation than Nancy's," Kathy said. "We have a bit of a cocoon situation in my family."

"What do you mean by that?"

"I mean we tend to isolate sometimes as a family. I have two children, a son named Alex who has LD and a daughter Christina who does not. Our big issue has been that Alex can't be happy for his sister for anything. Things have changed a bit lately and he's better about it now, but let me tell you what it was like. My daughter couldn't have sleepovers or a play-date because he would get mad if she had friends over. If she had good news, he would start storming around the house. For example, Christina was invited to a water park a while ago. During that same week, Alex was going away on a field trip with his school for two nights. Christina was fine with it. But when Alex found out she was going to the water park, he started yelling and screaming and running around the house and crying and saying, 'It's not fair!' Now remember, he said this even though he was also going away on a field trip too. She couldn't even be happy without him having a problem with it. They're very close, but he hurt her a lot because he couldn't get out of his own anger. I would say, 'Alex, you are hurting her. She's crying about this.' But it didn't seem to register. And it's not fair. She shouldn't have to temper her happiness for him."

"How old are they?"

"Christina is thirteen, Alex is twelve," Kathy said. "I was reading a book about NLD (non-verbal learning disabilities), and it said that most kids with NLD are at about 75% maturity level. So Alex is really at a level more typical of a nine year old. I tell that to Christina, and she said, 'But I didn't do that when I was nine either!' I try to talk to her about it and tell her she's not the only one he's doing it to. He has a hard time with the kids at school. He will say inappropriate things. I tell her it has less to do with her and so much more to do with him. We've always been open with her because she's pretty mature. She's empathetic and compassionate and she's pretty knowledgeable about this kind of thing."

"That doesn't always make it easier," I said.

"That's right. Sometimes she would just start crying because she can't take it anymore. It happened during that outburst over the water park. She started crying because he said he hated her. Of course, he doesn't hate her, but she really takes it hard. I tell her that he loves her more than anything, and he does – but he just can't be happy for her. He thinks everything is so much better for her. I tell him that he really has to get out of his world and think about other people sometimes, but it's very hard for him."

"After he calms down, is he remorseful?" I asked. "We sometimes see a lack of empathy in children with LD, or a tendency toward self-centeredness. Does he realize what he's done?"

"I don't know if he's truly remorseful, but he'll come to me and say he loves me. The trouble is, he doesn't say it to her. But having said all that, I should also tell you we have made some real progress lately. Alex's psychologist always told us he would eventually develop empathy for others and feel it enough to control his reactions. And thankfully, I think he has turned a corner."

"It is not uncommon to see self-centeredness and a lack of empathy in children with learning disabilities," I said. "I've had teachers in schools talk about this, wondering how to get past that. One way to get beyond it is teaching and reinforcing social skills. How did Alex turn the corner?"

"It was a simple thing. One day, while Christina was crying about Alex saying he hated her, she finally let him see her crying."

"She never did that before?"

"No. She either cried to me or on her own. Letting Alex see the real, honest impact his words were having on her was embarrassing for her, but it had amazing results. He has not said he hates her since then. I think he's becoming a little more mature in the way he deals with the natural inequities life gives each of us. He has learned to 'accept the no' when things don't go his way without screaming or running away. He has learned to accept when Christina goes to a friend's house or has a special event. Life has been so much better for us – and it's amazing when I think of how bad it was not so long ago."

MARLA
"LD is my 'normal'"

"I have two children, a girl and a boy. They both have LD but they were not diagnosed at the same time. When my daughter Karen was in kindergarten, I got blindsided in the middle of a parent teacher conference. The teacher proceeded to give us her version of a report card and I started to have this strange feeling that something was really wrong. I knew she was about to say something that would be difficult to hear, so I stopped her and asked her to tell us the bottom line. She said, 'Your daughter is having significant perceptual processing problems.' I had no prior experience with LD. I wasn't *getting* it. I didn't really understand what she meant by 'significant perceptual processing problems'. Even so, she probably saved my child that day. I brought Karen to be tested and I started to learn about LD to try to figure out what my beautiful, artsy child was up to. But it was complicated. It's *still* complicated. Along the way, her brother Josh, who is a couple of years behind her, was just fine – or so I thought. But here's what happened. I spent so much time worrying about Karen and being so grateful that Josh was OK, that when I saw a little sign of something going on with him, I wasn't sure I was right. My son's set of learning disabilities are completely opposite of my daughter's. Eventually I looked at my husband and said, 'Something is wrong with Josh.' I was still going through a lot with my daughter and I said, 'I don't have the energy to figure it out, but something's up.'

"What was his reaction?" I asked.

"He was floored. I delayed the testing by about six months. When I finally wanted to get him tested, the school refused to do it. Finally I told myself to trust my intuition and not let the school or anyone else tell me I was imagining things. But I was at a point where I had two children who were very close in age and who needed separate kinds of help and I didn't have a clue what to do about it. Eventually I got them into the Craig School and it really changed our lives. The bottom line is that I have two kids with completely different issues. I felt so guilty that I didn't get on his disabilities as soon as I got on hers, and I didn't even get on hers soon enough. The guilt was tremendous."

"And it doesn't get you anywhere," I said.

"That's exactly the conclusion I reached on my own. Feeling guilty over everything wasn't doing any good at all. It wasn't helping."

I asked Marla if having two children with LD led to the same kind of sibling issues experienced by the other mothers at the table.

"Over the years I've had to do a lot of navigating between my children," she said. "I've had to navigate between their disabilities and styles of learning. My two children love each other, and they are absolutely forbidden to tease each other about their disabilities."

"Do they ever do that?" I asked.

"Oh, sure. They try. For instance, if they get really mad, one might say, 'well, you don't know how to do this or that' — and that's when I put my foot down. They have had to learn to live with each other, and to live with their own challenges, and to embrace that and understand what it means. I introduced labels to them at different points because I knew things would come up and they would need to know how to explain their own disabilities. For the most part, they don't define themselves by their LD — and I don't want them to. Even so, I have to say that having two children with LD is my 'normal.' I don't know anything else. It's their 'normal' too. That's our family. And in my own variation on this sibling theme, I've had to help educate them to the point where she can understand him, and he can understand her."

SALLY
"Love is not time"

"I have to say this issue is a fairly easy one for me. My son Peter has LD and is my eldest child. He has two younger brothers. Peter has never wanted to be like them. At an early age we discovered that he had food allergies, so early on he was always the 'food allergy kid' and then he became the 'depressive kid' and then the 'LD kid,' but he never bought into those labels. He's Peter. He's happy being Peter. That is who he is. I think it must be more difficult when the siblings are closer in age and one is getting something the other one can't. I have a different take on the whole thing because I am completely intolerant of jealousy in the house. I always say, 'Love is not Time.' So yeah, Peter takes a lot more time because there are evaluations, there have been lawsuits, there have been doctor's offices, there have been all these different things going on — but not because I love him more. It's because I have to do that in order to get him through life."

"And the others understand that?" I asked.

"Yes," Sally said. "If they ask how come I spent four hours with Peter, I let them know from the very beginning that Peter needed four hours, and that's the end of it. If one of the others needed four hours, I would spend four hours with him. We do make a point of spending time with each one individually. When we decided to have children, the one thing that I always said was they were number one. They were the most important thing. These are the people I wanted in my life and they are the most important thing in my life. I think if you come to it with that perspective, you start giving the kids the time that they need at the time they need it."

"THANK YOU FOR LETTING ME COME WITH YOU"

Twins: One with Special Needs and One Without

Hearts entwined
Twenty fingers, twenty toes,
two sweet babies with cheeks of rose.
Born on the same day, two gifts from above,
lives entwined, two babies to love.

~Author Unknown

We have heard about the challenges associated with LD and sibling issues. Let's now turn our focus onto possible solutions to these challenges.

I spoke by telephone with Donna, a mother of twins. It's difficult to imagine a more vivid illustration of sibling togetherness than identical twins, but what happens when one twin is born with special needs and one without?

Donna lives in Austin, Texas. Her two sons, Thomas and Luka, were carried by a surrogate and are now nine and a half years old. Thomas was born with special needs, and his twin Luka was born without. Donna's husband has also been diagnosed with disabilities, so we can safely say that she is truly living on the frontline of the disabilities world.

I began by asking about Thomas' diagnosis.

"Autism," she said, "though I don't quite believe it. He never displayed many of the aspects of autism. Thomas is non-verbal but he always was, right from the beginning. The standard story with autism is that kids are developing normally and then one day they change and their speech is gone. That never happened with us. He was never developing normal speech. He communicates by sign language and a voice generation program on an iPad. It's called Sonoflex and it allows him to communicate."

"You have a unique take on the sibling issue as you have two children who are the exact same age, one with special needs and one without. Many parents could attribute difficulties to a difference in ages, but you can't do that."

"No. With us, the sibling issues are attributable to the simple fact that one has a disability and one does not. It's very frustrating for Luka, and most of his frustrations come from low self-esteem and having a special needs sibling."

"In what ways does his self esteem suffer?" I asked.

"First of all it stems from the fact that he gets less time spent on him than is spent on his twin. I always have to work with his brother, especially since his father can't do it. His father doesn't get it."

"Why not?"

"Because he also has disabilities. My husband was diagnosed with Aspergers and mild Tourettes. He wasn't diagnosed until after the children were born."

"How did you first find out Thomas had special needs?"

"I noticed something as early as three months. I noticed Thomas's reactions were different than Luka's. At first, Thomas was the larger twin. He was the one to hit developmental milestones first. But he was also the one whose movements were a bit spastic sometimes. He would cry excessively. Once I took him outside in the sun to see if that would help with the crying and he instantly buried his face in my shoulder. He couldn't handle the sunlight. He is very sensitive to a lot of things. His appearance was a little different too. Even his skin looked different. He felt very soft. That was a result of lower muscle tone. Our first pediatrician kept saying that Thomas was developing normally, and when I expressed concerns he would say I worried too much because I was an older parent (forty five years old) and overzealous in comparing him to his twin."

"I had the exact same thing happen to me with my pediatrician," I said. "I remember taking Allegra in to see the pediatrician for an eye exam because I knew there was something wrong but I couldn't put my finger on it. She took the exam and got every single letter wrong. He still said there was nothing wrong with her."

"There were also food allergies with Thomas."

"That was the same with Allegra too. I often hear this in connection with children with special needs. Allegra was allergic to everything, dairy, chocolate, you name it. To this day, she has a very limited diet. What have been the greatest challenges for you, as far as sibling issues go? Challenges for you, for Luka and for Thomas?"

"It's difficult to say what is challenging for Thomas. He seems pretty satisfied with the whole situation. He's really affectionate with his brother. He's very confident that if he goes to Luka for a hug, he's going to get a hug. Luka, on the other hand, clearly goes through times when he feels that he is second place after Thomas. He feels Thomas is more important because things are always about going to Thomas's therapy and doctor appointments and working with him and that leaves little time for Luka and, frankly, due to the cost of therapy, no extra money to do the things Luka might want to do."

"Are you aware he is feeling these things while he is feeling them?"

"Oh, yes, absolutely. "

"Does he vocalize it? Or are you intuitively aware of it?"

"Both," Donna said. "I am intuitively aware of it but during the past year he has been vocalizing it more."

"Before he started to vocalize it, what would he do?"

"He would tend to withdraw and say he was okay. Even if we asked him if he wanted to do something with us, he would say, 'No, that's okay, I just want to be by myself.' Whenever I hear Luka say he wants to be alone, I know there is a problem."

"Is the problem generally because he doesn't feel enough attention is being paid to him?"

"Yes, and it breaks my heart to see him like that. I tell him I understand what he is going through, and he is astute enough and self-aware enough to say,

'I think I just want more attention.' He says that at nine years old. Last week he said to me, 'I may talk all cool and tough but I'm fragile and easy to break like an egg.' He realizes that he wants as much attention as he can get. He gets attention from me, but he doesn't get it from his father. That's what's tough."

"Does Thomas get attention from his father?"

"No. None at all."

"Both boys don't get attention because your husband is not capable of giving attention? Is that right?"

"Yes. In fact, he would be hard-pressed to give attention even if both kids were verbal. He has always been better with Luka because he gets more response from Luka. When Thomas was four months old I told my husband that if he didn't communicate to him, he would never talk. And look where we are. It's certainly not all his fault, of course. There are physical things in play. Obviously there is a predisposition, but it is still very rough. So now on top of the emotional barrier, we've got the language barrier. In all this time, my husband hasn't learned sign language and still hasn't learned to use the voice generation program."

I asked Donna if she could remember any times when Thomas' disability became an issue with people outside the family.

"Oh yes, it happens all the time," she said. "We just had an incident involving a birthday party. We have some local friends who also have twins. We met the day before my boys turned three years old so we've known them for about six years. We were introduced by a mutual friend and they came to the boys' birthday party the next day. Their kids were, and have been, my children's best friends for the past six years. They have been very supportive of both of my sons and I frequently have had their kids over for sleepovers. Luka would often go to their house for sleepovers too. They made it clear that they weren't comfortable having Thomas for sleepovers and I understood that because he's a kid with no fear of heights and doesn't understand safety issues. So that was okay. They moved out of the neighborhood about a year and a half ago but we stayed in touch and the kids still play together. Thomas has really had a close relationship with them. So her twins were having their birthday party last month and when I got the email invitation it was simply a directive to drop Luka off. It didn't mention Thomas at all. When I responded, I asked if the wording of her email meant that Thomas was not invited. She told me yes, he was not invited. She thought it was too much. The party was going to be outside and there was going to be water and a lot of kids, so she thought it best that Thomas didn't come. It was really a heart-wrenching experience for me. She was oblivious, and still doesn't understand why I was upset by the fact that she excluded Thomas. She maintains that she has always been very inclusive and supportive of him but she doesn't believe he belongs in a public setting, even though he has been to every birthday party since they met all those years ago and has never caused a problem."

"Is he disruptive?"

"No, not at all."

"So if he goes to a party, he's not going to be running around and scream-ing."

"No. He never has. Never. And this is one reason why I've always fought the autism label. He doesn't have tantrums. He is a very happy child. He is generally a very easy kid."

"Did Luka know any of this was going on?"

"Luka knew it. He told me that he still wanted to go to the party but he didn't like his friends' mother any more."

"Did he go to the party?"

"He did. And I had to bite my tongue and take him. I think what bothered me the most was that she didn't preface it all by saying that she didn't think it would be the best environment for Thomas or that it might be a little too much for him the way she did when there were sleepovers and a lack of adult supervision. As I say, I understood her reluctance to have Thomas sleep over because of safety issues, but this was an event with lots of people during the day. She only sent the email asking me to drop Luka off and telling me I didn't need to stay if I didn't want to."

"Does Luka know why she didn't want Thomas to go?"

"Absolutely, and he was upset by it. He was so upset he didn't really enjoy going to the party. From the time we got there he wanted to leave."

"It's awful to single out a child like that," I said.

"Sometimes other children will ask Luka what is wrong with Thomas, why he doesn't talk, why he doesn't play with them."

"What is Luka's response?"

"He'll say, 'Oh, he has special needs but he's as smart as everyone else, and he uses his iPad to talk.' He's very matter of fact about it."

"And what about Thomas? Did he know about the party?"

"I didn't talk to him about it. In general he becomes frustrated if one of us takes Luka somewhere by himself, so he clearly wants to be included. Even so, it's tough to get into difficult topics when you're using an iPad to communicate."

"How does Luka communicate with him?"

"Luka just talks to him. Certain things, he signs to him."

"They communicate in their own way."

"Yes. They have a great relationship. Luka can walk up to him and hold out his arms and Thomas jumps into his arms and wraps his legs around him. Once Luka said to him, 'Thank you for giving up being born alone and letting me come with you.'"

"What a beautiful thing to say."

"Luka is the only person who Thomas ever kisses."

"Does he kiss you?"

"Recently I had to be hospitalized for a couple of days. We took both kids to the ER with us and Thomas crawled into bed and lay on top of me, looked right into my eyes and smiled as he stroked my cheek. I held out my hand to him and he kissed me for the first time ever."

"That was quite a moment I'm sure."

"It certainly was."

"Getting back to the party, it sounds to me that mother simply didn't understand Thomas, even after knowing him all these years."

"Yes. It's even more difficult with people who don't know him very well. Thomas doesn't look like he has disabilities so people aren't sure what is going on. Once at a local gym, he took a toy out of another child's hand. I was with him and took it from him and gave it right back to the girl. Her father exploded and started going on about how Thomas should know better and how I was such a lousy parent. I apologized again and explained that Thomas had special needs and that the toy happened to be one of his favorites, but the man kept yelling at us. I took Thomas's hand and we removed ourselves from the situation. Then the child's mother began screaming at us too, so we left to go to our car. She followed us outside, still screaming. When we were at the car I explained once again that he has special needs and that we'd already apologized twice and we were leaving."

"What was she saying?"

"The same thing the father said, that I was a terrible parent and he needed some control, and I wasn't keeping him in line and he needs to be disciplined.

When I got ready to leave, the last thing she said was 'He doesn't have any more special needs than I do.' Because, again, he doesn't look like he has special needs. It seems to me that people with invisible special needs have it worse than those with physical disabilities."

"Many people simply do no understand. They need a visual cue."

"On the rare occasions when we go a restaurant, we get stares and negative head shaking every time because the kids are sitting at the table using the iPad. People are thinking we just want to pacify them while we ignore them and talk. They don't know that Thomas is non-verbal and that the device is used for speech generation programs."

"Can we turn to things you have done that have helped Luka?"

"The first thing I would say is that we need to recognize that siblings need to grieve for the loss of the normal brother or sister. This loss is something they feel acutely. Luka will say every day that he feels lesser than his friends because he doesn't have a normal sibling and because Thomas can't play with him at the same level. We can work with them on doing the same activities but Thomas is not always going to be interested. If we sit down to watch a movie, he goes off on his own. A lot of time we have to plan what we do around Thomas because we know he's not going to care about most things. His interests lie elsewhere and that's not going to change. The best we can do is make an effort to find that place where things overlap and where there is mutual interest and where they can sit side by side and do the same thing. Even then, its rough for Luka because we have to adapt many activities for Thomas. For instance, if we're building a Lego project, my focus is always split between playing with Luka and teaching Thomas, because they're not in the same place."

"You said Luka says he feels 'lesser than his friends' or inadequate every day. Do you mean he says it quite often? Or do you really mean every day?"

"Yes, I really do mean every day. He really feels a lack of close friendships. We live in a neighborhood where there are not a lot of kids so he doesn't have other children to play with. But it's not only that: it's the fact that he can't have a typical friendship with his twin. He feels that relationship, he feels the bond, but they don't have that back and forth where Thomas is interested in doing the same things he is. Even in those rare occasions when Thomas is interested, he can't participate on the same level with Luka. We don't know if he ever will."

"Does Luka feel a sense of guilt over having a brother with special needs?"

"Oh yes. We've got no sibling rivalry here. The situation saddens Luka but he doesn't have any resentment. He understands why I have to work with Thomas, but he feels a profound need to grieve for the loss of his 'normal' twin, and sometimes wonders whether something he did as a baby caused Thomas's special needs. He is always asking me if he did something wrong when he was a baby or before they were born that caused his brother's disabilities."

"And what do you say in that case?"

"I say absolutely not, and that there is nothing he could have done to hurt anybody. I tell him he's a great brother and that I can't imagine a better brother for Thomas."

"Does it help?"

"Yes, but it's still difficult though. At times his feelings about this are so debilitating that it almost seems like he is more the one with special needs than Thomas is. He is so upset by it, and worries about it, and truly does grieve for the loss every single day. We do too. At least, I do."

"I think all parents do to one extent or another," I said. "It is a long process, coming to terms with having a child with disabilities."

"In some ways, Luka picked up on Thomas's disabilities before anyone. I remember when they were very young before Thomas was crawling...Luka would get Thomas what we called his lovey blanket because he knew Thomas couldn't do it on his own. So he realized even then that there was a difference, but I think that was at an instinctual level. At a more intellectual level, he's been aware of Thomas as having special needs since they were about four, when we began having to see so many therapists and doctors. We redefine things as progress is being made and always focus on what Thomas *can* do rather than what he can't do. And again, we try to engage both of the boys in things they can do side by side, though as Luka says, 'The best I can do is get him to watch a video with me, or watch me play Minecraft.' Luka is a very reasonable kid. He is unfailingly kind to Thomas. He is always cheering him on. Even so there are times when Luka will maintain that he doesn't deserve to be happy or that he's a bad kid."

"Why does he feel that?"

"Because he feels left out that his friends have normal siblings and he can't play with Thomas on the same level even though they're twins. He feels guilty about being resentful about that. He's also lonely because our neighborhood isn't full of kids."

"What efforts do you make to help this situation?

"We try to do our share of Cub Scouts and summer camps with him, but it's not the same as being able to spend time with the same friends again and again. It's the close friendships he craves. He sees friends as a replacement for what he can't get with Thomas, but unfortunately we don't have enough children living around us. It's difficult."

I heard a voice in the background, muffled and high, say something to Donna. "Oh thank you," she said to someone else in the room. "I love you too, sweet-pea. Mommy's on the phone right now. I'll talk to you in a little bit."

"Was that Luka?" I asked.

"Yes. He came in to tell me he loves me. And by the way, that's another thing my own mother noticed really early on. He wasn't getting it from Thomas, so he focused more intensely on me. She said, 'I don't know why he feels he has to tell you he loves you so much.' At the time I didn't know why my mother would even bring it up or see it as something of a problem. He's a nice, loving child – so that's what he does. He tells me he loves me and I tell him I love him. We didn't hear that in my family when I was growing up so I intended to do things differently with my kids. So he tells me he loves me all the time."

"Do you think that has been helpful?"

"Yes, I do. It opens up more lines of communication because it helps him be freer to talk, not only to me, but to anyone about how he feels. I think that is very important."

"I do too," I said. "We have seen over and over again that much of the problem involved with sibling issues comes from a lack of communication."

"I feel it is always important to ask Luka how he is doing or, for example, if he understands why we need to take Thomas to therapy. It's also important to involve him. It was important for him to learn to sign and to help with Thomas's therapy. It's a huge thing and it definitely helps Luka. In fact, this year he requested to go to Thomas's school instead of the one he had been going to."

"Thomas does not go to a school for special needs children?"

"No. He goes to a mainstream school but one that can accommodate children with special needs. I felt Luka was old enough to make the decision to go there, so they are now going to the same school. It's a much smaller school and I like the administration better. I think they have a much better handle on instructing children with special needs and the way things work in special needs families. Having a child with special needs affects the entire family. There is no way it doesn't."

"It always does," I agreed. "LD and special needs do not stop at the classroom door. If nothing else, they can cause an unexpected financial burden. This applies to sibling issues as well, as money spent on requirements of special needs takes away from money spent on the child without the disability."

"Exactly. When I was growing up, my family went out to dinner at least once a week. But with special needs, so little is covered by insurance. You go for allergy testing and that is $7,000 down the drain. Every time we go to a therapy session it's a $25 or $35 co-pay. My husband lost his job back in November and when we lost his insurance through that company, we learned Thomas's speech therapy sessions were going to cost $140 each, three times weekly. It's rough enough when you are employed, but when you are unemployed, it's incredibly difficult."

"How does that affect Luka?"

"It's a lot of stress for him. He's not a very greedy kid. But he wants to have family experiences. He would like to do things with us. We would love to take them on vacations. The last vacation we took was to get allergy testing for Thomas."

"Oh Donna, it sounds like you have a difficult situation, but you are handing it well. You being so open about it and so accepting of your situation and your understanding of Luka's needs is really impressive. I commend you for that. Allegra has gone through life basically happy and unaware of all the turmoil involved with dealing with her LD. It sounds like you have the same situation with Thomas."

"Oh yes. Thomas is a happy camper, all the time."

"I am happy to hear that you know that about Thomas and can spare some thought and time for Luka."

"It is important for me to do that. I have to listen to Luka all the time. Even when he's not saying anything, I have to check in with him to find out what he's thinking and doing. I'll give you an example. Last Saturday, Luka was frustrated the entire day because we had therapy and all kinds of different things going on for Thomas and he wasn't able to do what he wanted. These frustrations tend to come out at bedtime. I spent all this time preparing him for bed, giving him an hour notice, then a half hour, ten minutes, five minutes, and so on. This is at his request. He likes the ten minute and five minute warnings. Last Saturday, once the warnings passed, he just couldn't handle all the frustration still inside, and so he ran away. He just took off."

"Where did he go?"

"He ran down the block. The trouble is it was very late. My husband was already in bed. He got up and stood watch out front in case Luka came back, so I took Thomas with me. He sat in the back seat while I drove around for over an hour searching for Luka. I can't even begin to tell you how frightening it was."

"And he did this because he was frustrated?"

"He didn't want to go to bed. I kept trying to reason with him, and I think this is where a lot of the frustration and stress comes into play. He can't always isolate what is bothering him. When he can't handle it, then he acts out. It's the only time he does."

"It's hard to isolate what you are feeling sometimes. I think everyone has that problem from time to time. Overall, Luka sounds like a pretty cool kid. How do you feel about how he's adjusting, and what you've done and what you've tried to do with him? How do you feel about Luka's future?"

"I think he's going to be fine. He's so bright. He's so articulate. He's receptive to working with anything we do. He's smart enough to know when something isn't working for him. For instance, there is a child across the street who is visiting his grandmother. She sent him over here to play and Luka gave it a try but the boy upset him and made him feel bad and Luka doesn't want to be around him. I think it's the greatest thing that he is not so desperate for a friend that he's willing to put up with somebody who makes him feel bad. He doesn't deserve that. That's the main thing I worry about with him. I want to get past this feeling that he doesn't deserve to be happy, or doesn't deserve anything better. Because he does. This child could not be a better brother to Thomas. They are twins, but in some ways he considers himself an older brother to Thomas. And with the constant 'I love you' stuff, I think he says it because he knows Thomas can't."

"Thomas can't say it to you?"

"Right. Thomas can't say he loves me. I think Luka is trying to make up for that. By the way, I should tell you if you wanted to talk to Luka about any of this, he is open to it. He knows I am talking to you."

"I think that would be great."

Donna asked Luka to come to the phone. After we said hello and introduced ourselves, I asked him if we could talk a little about his brother Thomas and how he felt about having a brother with special needs. "How has that affected you?" I asked.

"It's pretty hard," Luka said.

"In what way?"

"It's pretty hard every day because it's sad that Thomas has special needs."

"Do you feel protective of your brother?" I asked, and I realized Luka mistook 'protective' for 'protected' when he said he sometimes doesn't feel protected because of his brother. "In what way?" I asked.

"When Thomas is mad," he said. "The other day I was guarding the door when he wanted to go outside and he pushed me and I fell into the shoe basket."

"And what is it like to communicate with your brother?" I asked. "Do you think you can talk to him better than most other people can?"

"Yes, but sometimes it's hard because he doesn't understand me."

"You know your brother requires a lot of services and therapy. Does that ever make you feel left out?"

"Sometimes," Luka said. "And it's hard sometimes because Thomas is so happy all the time and he's having so much fun."

"He's having so much fun and you're not?"

"Yes. And my dad has Aspergers and that makes it more hard."

"So even though Thomas needs all the therapy, he's always happy. Is that irritating for you?"

"Sometimes, yes. It makes me wonder why he's happy, especially when I'm not happy. That usually happens because I don't get to see my friends. The kid who lived across the street for the summer used to come over. I used to play with him but I kind of don't like him. He's kind of inappropriate sometimes."

"Well, we all have inappropriate friends at times, so I know what you're going through," I said. "Luka, it sounds to me like you really understand your brother has special needs and that your mother is doing her best. You're a really good brother and I can tell that you love your brother even with all the difficulties. I think it's wonderful you are helping out so much."

"I know Thomas loves me too but he can't talk," Luka said. "He can't show it. But he can hug me and high five with me."

"That's how he shows how he feels about you. It sounds like you have a very special relationship."

"I think we do."

"I'm so glad for both of you."

Luka passed the phone back to his mother who laughed and said, "He's my sweetheart, I tell you. They both are."

"It's so nice that he's so aware of everything at this age. It doesn't make it easier for him, but I think it will make things smoother for him down the road. I also think Luka is very lucky to have you as a mother, and I think he's going to be fine. In my experience, when adults of siblings with disabilities have troubles about this, it's almost always due to a lack of communication when they were younger. It sounds like you've got that under control."

"After Luka ran away last week I knew something had to be done. We had a therapist talk to him and do a thorough assessment. She asked a lot of really pointed questions to discover if there were any signs of mental illness, or if Luka was just having trouble dealing with everyday issues. The latter is what she came up with: that he's just having a little trouble dealing with everyday issues. Overall, he's perfectly fine. He's just has trouble coping sometimes."

"Well, it *is* difficult for him sometimes. What did he tell you when you found him after he had run away?"

"After I found him — which was a huge relief — I spent much of the time driving beside him with the window down, talking to him."

"And did it work?"

"Oh yes. When we finally got home my husband asked Luka why he didn't stop when he saw me, and he said 'Oh, we were just having a nice stroll in the moonlight.'"

"So that's a little bump in the road, but overall, it sounds to me like your two sibling twins, Luka and Thomas, are as loving and close to each other as they could be."

"They are," Donna said. "At the boys' school they've got several different Special Ed classes. Each one has a number of children without special needs who come in on a regular basis to work with the kids, and they are trained by the teachers. They're given certain protocols to use, so if they're dealing with kids with Aspergers or Autism, for example, they're taught to make eye contact with them or tap them on the shoulder if they lose attention. They call them buddies. Luka is one of the buddies. He is in Thomas's class."

"And how is he doing with that?" I asked. "Does he like it?

"He loves it."

"And does he deal specifically with Thomas?"

"He does, yes. And it's a good thing for him because that was the main reason why he wanted to switch schools. He wanted to be with his brother."

"We hear so many stories of children not wanting to spend time with their brother or sister with special needs. It's nice to hear about Luka and Thomas."

"They both take the bus to school, and I hear from the bus driver and the aides on the bus how terrific it is to see them together, and that Luka is always so loving with Thomas and can't wait to be with him at the end of the day."

To recap, let's look at some of the concrete steps that Donna took to help the situation:

- Communication. Luka never had any doubt his brother had special needs. Every question he had was answered to the best of his mother's ability. All children will have questions about a sibling with special needs: whether or not they express those questions is another matter. If you as a parent feel you cannot answer your child's questions, the therapist or pediatrician working with your disabled child will be able to help.

- Listening. Luka always felt free to discuss his feelings. His questions, his fears, his sadness; all his thoughts and emotions were validated. None were ever dismissed or belittled. Yes, he has the occasional bout of frustration and he acts out on that (such as the running away episode), but for the even then, he is allowed to freely air those frustrations.

- Honoring the Feelings. None of Luka's thoughts and emotions were dismissed or belittled. Regardless of how "out there" or mistaken he might be, his mother always took those feelings seriously.

- Inclusive Environment. Luka was included in many of the therapeutic measures taken for his brother's benefit. He learned to communicate, everything was explained to him, and all efforts were made to include him as a part of the family with responsibilities toward his brother.

STEPPING OUT OF THE SHADOW

Teenage Brothers and LD

*I*first met Debra when I was asked to speak at a school in New Jersey. After my talk, I met informally with a group of mothers outside the auditorium and mentioned this new project focused on sibling issues. Debra told us about a college essay written by her son Mark, the second of her three boys. Mark was diagnosed with LD and ADD (without Hyperactivity) when he was in second grade. Learning disabilities brought the usual challenges and difficulties into Mark's school and home life, and for many years, he felt he lived in the shadow of his older, very accomplished brother, Chris. Mark's essay was a turning point in his image of himself, and the moment when he truly stopped comparing himself to his brother. He has given us permission to include his essay at the end of this chapter, but I would first like to share Debra's thoughts on her sons and their relationship.

Here is her story:

I have three children, all boys. My oldest son is Chris, who is twenty-two. The middle son, Mark, is the one with learning disabilities. He is twenty now. My youngest son is Matthew, age sixteen.

When Mark was in second grade, I realized he couldn't memorize a lot of sight words. He was really struggling. When I asked him a question, he would get a look that I called 'the blank page.' He couldn't recall a thing. He wasn't visualizing what he needed to visualize, as if there was nothing there. I wasn't sure what it was. When you ask a question, you can usually see a child visually spell a word in their mind. Mark wasn't doing that. I went to the school and they kept putting it off and telling me it was developmental, but I knew it was something more. Early in third grade, I got him tested outside the school. He was diagnosed with learning disabilities and ADD without hyperactivity. He has no recall. He does not memorize. There were a lot of processing problems. Information would go in but it didn't come out. I went to the school with the results, which caused a huge problem because they wanted me to have him tested through them. I told them I would have done that but they kept telling me there was nothing wrong and that it was developmental. They should have done the testing themselves: it was their responsibility. Because they wouldn't do it, I took it upon myself to get the testing done, and I didn't even know what I was testing for. The only thing I knew was that there was something wrong, but I had no idea what it was. I wasn't getting answers from the school. He was struggling and it was getting worse and worse and his self esteem was way down. He was only in third grade but he couldn't even do the spelling words, and as adept as I was at getting things done, I didn't know that I could have pulled him out of the public school and put him in another school.

Nobody told me I could do that. I probably should have stumbled upon it in all of my research but I didn't. So the school issues were the first of many big problems associated with LD...and I have to say, he is a junior in college and I'm still dealing with it. I'm still trying to get him to pass one class.

Another issue was Mark's relationship with his brothers, especially his older brother Chris. If you were to speak to Chris, I don't think that he would say he was treated unfairly. If anything, he was not so much bothered by any sense of unfair treatment as he was by the impact of Mark's learning disabilities on the family as a whole. His LD affected the family dynamic. If he was moody or if he had a problem, it would consume the entire family. For example, let's say Mark didn't do well on a test or wasn't invited to a party because he wasn't part of a certain social group, when he walked in the door, his mood would take over the whole family. Everything always seemed to focus around Mark and everyone would be affected, and that most definitely includes me. I might even say it *especially* affected me.

My relationship with Mark was the worst. As much as I was the advocate, and have always been his advocate, and am *still* his advocate, my relationship with him was the most difficult. I would overreact to his mood or I would try to get him into a better frame of mind, but I'm the one he unloaded on. I'm the one that he would get upset with. We've had to work through that over the years. Chris would say I spent a lot of time helping Mark, but even more, I believe he would say there were some things Mark could get away with that he couldn't — behavioral issues, for example. Or Mark might say things that Chris would never be able to say. Things come easy to Chris. He always got As, always did well in school. Mark struggled with everything. That became a problem between the two of them. Mark didn't understand and resented Chris.

Chris, on the other hand, was not resentful and never said, 'look what you're doing for him.' He just receded into his own world. Mark and Chris were not close in those early years after Mark's diagnosis. They were only two years apart and played the same sports, but there was no camaraderie between the two. Now there is, but not back then. It's also interesting that we never used the words 'learning disabilities' in the home. For example, I never said to the other boys, "You have to feel bad for Mark because he has a learning disability." I guess I shielded them from it; but in some ways, that jeopardized my relationship with Mark because it made me the 'bad guy.'

I was the one who got the call from school and I would have to go to Mark and ask why he didn't do his homework, or why he didn't do something they had asked him to do. I believe the schools are wrong when they make the family responsible for everything. That's where some of the problems come in. It becomes so horrible within the household — you know, they always called me to tell me that he's not doing his homework and I kept asking why they weren't taking responsibility for it. They were making him accountable to me rather than the teachers and that made for some heated arguments between Mark and me. In eighth grade, I called all of his teachers together and said, "I can't have this role anymore with him because it's killing my relationship with my son. He no longer wants to come home because I'm the bad guy. It's also killing my relationship with my other children because there is so much tension between Mark and me. The school needs to take more accountability."

They didn't. And that was a problem.

There continued to be a lot of tension between Mark and me, which left the rest of the family relatively unscathed. I took the brunt of it, but I did it on purpose. I didn't want the other two boys to be resentful toward Mark. I didn't want them to be involved with all this, so I would try to relieve the tension in the house by letting things slide with Mark…which I shouldn't have.

I believed he should have been accountable and that I should have come down hard on him, but I didn't always do that. I would back off to avoid making the problems worse. Eventually I did do a few things that really helped. I found resources outside of the house. I took him to counseling. I took him to three different people who could help him learn skills at school. And most helpful of all, I found someone he could talk to, someone who wasn't *me*. That took the pressure off both of us. He and I talk a lot about what happened then. He tells me I loved him too much.

Chris and Mark continued to have problems, mostly because Mark always felt he needed to keep up with his older brother. This was a real problem. I kept saying, 'Mark, you don't need to keep up with Chris or anybody else. You just need to keep up with Mark.' But there was a point in his life when that did not make any sense to him at all. For instance, his freshman year in high school was really bad. He was in the same school with his older brother who everyone loved. There was actually a teacher who looked at an essay Mark handed in and said, 'Your brother would never have handed this in'. Those sorts of things would completely destroy Mark. It hurt his relationship with his brother. I confronted the teacher about it, and he said, 'but I really loved Chris.' I said 'Even so, you can't say that to Mark. Mark doesn't need to live up to Chris's expectations. He has to live up to Mark's expectations, whatever they are.' But the teacher wasn't alone. We went through that kind of situation over and over. We went through it in sports. We went through it academically. For Mark, everything ended up being about Chris, but for me, it could never be all about Chris. No matter what it was, I tried to make sure it was also about Mark because I never wanted him to feel badly about himself. So no matter what Chris accomplished, I somehow needed Mark to accept it and feel good about Chris' accomplishment, which rarely happened.

Once in a while there was a small success. There was a time we went on a college search for Chris and he got accepted into Northeastern. I decided we should also show Mark some colleges while we were up there and, for once, that turned out to be a good thing. That was when Mark finally realized that he was never going to be like Chris and that he shouldn't want to be. I didn't know any of this until nine months later when he wrote a college essay called *Stepping Out of the Shadow*. (Included at the end of this chapter)

I always say to the boys that they have choices in life and they need to focus on what they do best. When it comes to children with LD, parents need to find the one thing that the child is passionate about and help that child move toward it. From the time Mark was two years old, he was outside pushing the plastic lawn mower. He is now an environmental science major at U. Mass Lowell. I knew his passions would lead to working outside. He wasn't going to be sitting in a cubicle. He wasn't going to be doing math. I kept pushing him toward his passion. I looked for and provided opportunities whenever I could, and continually encouraged him. I still continue to do that.

I have always tried to help Mark map out the resources to help him get through. For instance, he took a calculus course over the summer but he failed it. He then took an online course – he's taking the test tomorrow and the school may accept the results. One of the problems is that there is still a dynamic that goes on with Mark that involves the stigma associated with LD. The stigma still drives him crazy at twenty years old.

He doesn't want to go to the school and get the accommodations that he needs to be able to get extra time on tests. He doesn't want to not feel 'normal.' He and I have gone through therapy over this. We've gone separately and we've gone together. I have tried to make him understand that it's not the end of the world to have LD, but it's so difficult for him. He said to me just yesterday, 'I don't want to take this test tomorrow.' I asked him why, what's the worst thing that could happen? He said, 'I could fail it and feel stupid again.' He's twenty years old. I've been hearing the same thing from him since he was in 5th grade.

My other sons, Chris and Matt, know I'm still dealing with Mark's issues. They see it happening. But if they had similar issues, I'd do the same for them, and they know that too. They're happy if Mark is happy. That goes back to what I said earlier about Mark's moods affecting the family. They want him to be happy. It's much better for everyone. And Chris and Mark are very close now. Chris will say to me, 'He's so much more social and happier because he's happier with himself.'

STEPPING OUT OF THE SHADOW

by
Mark

A shadow is a region of darkness where light is blocked. I should know, because I spent a long time in a shadow. For much of my life, I lived in the shadow of my older brother, Chris. Two years older than me, Chris was a tough act to follow. He was a star athlete, a top student, and an all-around popular person. Even if it was unintentional, people always compared me to my big brother. Teachers, classmates, and parents of friends had certain expectations of me simply because of who Chris was.

The size of a shadow changes over time. During the first two years of high school, the shadow I dwelt in was very big. Chris was an upperclassman at our high school, and I was just starting out. I was struggling with a learning disability and low self-esteem. I was apathetic, unhappy, isolated from my family, and completely uninterested in my school work. A teacher actually said to me, "Chris would not have turned this paper in." Why should I care, if there was just no way I would measure up to my brother?

During my sophomore year, Chris was accepted to a prestigious university in Boston. My family and I traveled to "Bean town" to see my brother's new school, and we made an appointment to tour another college while we were there, so that I could start my own college search. I soon found myself on a baseball field in the middle of Boston. On my right was the top-tier school where Chris would be going. On my left was the school where I could expect to be accepted based on my grades at the time. Right side: excitement, success, confidence, happiness, light. Left side: dreariness, mediocrity, lifelessness, darkness...a school where shadows are expected to go.

I stood on that baseball field and watched my own shadow lengthen with the sun's rays. I knew that I wanted something more than what was on my left and something different than what was on my right. I wanted to step out of the shadow that I had been in so long and find a place where my strengths would be recognized, a place where I was respected for who I was, a place so filled with light that shadows could not even be seen.

My realization led to a complete turnaround in my personality and overall well being. I started to think more about my own interests, instead of comparing myself to Chris, as so many others had done. I joined community groups that cared about the issues that were important to me. I changed my hairstyle and my wardrobe to reflect my new positive attitude and energy. I indulged my passion for the outdoors and began to volunteer with an environmental agency. I learned about what I could expect as an environmental science major, and I became inspired. My motivation and drive led to academic success; I had started high school with a 2.6 GPA, and I now have a 3.9.

As I look back on the changes that occurred in my life over the past year and a half, I see that my brother's shadow may have been something I helped to create. I realize now that I am a strong person with my own ideas, dreams and ambitions. I respect Chris for what he has accomplished, and over the last year, I have come to recognize what a role model he has been to me.

We have become the best of friends and we now relate to each other as equals with distinct interests and inspirations. Our lives are both filled with light; any shadow that may have once existed is now too small to be seen.

Adult Siblings
The lingering effects of LD

When siblings grow up, most rivalries (especially the petty ones) disappear. Things that used to consume us, vital things such as "why did she get a red sweater for Christmas and I got a blue one?" don't seem quite as important anymore. Siblings of individuals with disabilities generally find their hurt feelings, their anger, and jealousies diminish as well. It can therefore come as a surprise when one discovers that some of these feelings do not completely disappear. Parents can be astounded to learn this, and even the adult child can feel a bit of shock and even embarrassment to realize they are *still* holding onto ancient grudges that should have been abandoned long ago.

It is all too easy to say these adults should get over it and move on. Most can, and most do, but for some, this resentment continues to gnaw away at their family relationships and their own self-esteem. We may wonder how a grown man or woman can be so affected by what they perceived as slights or unfair treatment years ago. Surely the time has come to move on, to let bygones be bygones, and to just 'get over it'.

Sometimes that is far easier said than done.

Recently, I was scrolling through an online chat group that asked people if they had had any experience with twins, one with a disability and one without. One of the respondents wrote this (quoted as written):

"My husband is a 43 year old fraternal twin. He also has a 47 year old brother who is 'normal' like my husband. My husband's twin brother was born with major physical and mental health problems, had multiple surgeries for two months before even coming home. The handicapped twin is at the forever age of an II year old boy. He takes daily medication and his diet is constantly monitored. My husband who was born without any physical or mental disabilities was treated as a middle child instead of the other twin. He was left at school without rides. Forgotten. He was teased about his twin brother riding the special bus, in the special class, and some hinted that he, too, was a special needs kid. The older 47 year old brother dismissed the twins completely and grew up acting as if he was an only child. My husband lived his life in the shadows, never making waves, constant disappointments and not a lot of self confidence. To the mothers out there that may have a similar or same situation, Get help!! Find a way to show the same attention to all your children. Get help for them on how to live with a special needs sibling!"

We will now hear from adults without LD who are working professionals, living in the world, some with families of their own, but who are still affected in one way or another by a sister or brother with LD or a related disorder. They are all men and women who know their past difficulties should all be "water under the bridge" but have been unable to fully remove enough obstacles to keep the water flowing as freely as it might.

"WHY CAN'T YOU HEAR
WHAT I'M SAYING?"

Melanie

*S*oon after my daughter's diagnosis of LD, I met another young mother
named Jennifer who also had a daughter with LD. We formed an instant
bond: she was the first person I opened up to about Allegra's challenges and she
did the same with me about her daughter Hannah. The two girls were the same
age and had similar interests and we related to each others' experiences in ways
I never could with others in my circle of friends.

Jennifer spent an inordinate amount of time with Hannah and her various
challenges in school and at home. I was doing the same with Allegra so I perfectly understood her reasons. Jennifer had a second daughter named Melanie
and had nothing but praise for this bright and happy younger child. As the
years passed and Melanie went from success to success, I heard only praise from
Jennifer and how proud she was of her daughter's achievements – especially
when Melanie graduated from Columbia School of Journalism in two years.
Hannah, on the other hand, became a source of true anguish and worry. She

got through school but careened from crisis to crisis in her personal life, nearly all a result of her learning disabilities. Whenever Jennifer began to talk of one of Melanie's achievements, the conversation quickly veered into familiar territory: "What am I going to do about Hannah?" or "I couldn't sleep last night, worrying about Hannah." Any enjoyment she might have had in Melanie's success was over-layered with anxiety for her eldest daughter. I wondered if these worries were expressed only to me and a few other close friends or if they had spilled over into her family life. I later learned they did.

Jennifer was diagnosed with breast cancer in the late 1990s and died after a long and valiant struggle. It was a devastating loss for her husband, her friends and, especially, her two daughters – Hannah (the child with learning disabilities) and Melanie, about seven years younger.

I recently sat down with Melanie to talk about this. The trip down memory lane was a difficult one. She seemed to feel all over again the same bumps and twists and turns that had caused her so much anguish so many years before. The feelings lie close to the surface, and for Melanie, they come with a sense that there will never be true closure.

I began by reminding her that we had once talked about all this and that she told me then that she felt that she never received the same adulation as her sister, no matter what she did or how much she accomplished.

"I think in my case it was less about getting adulation than the fact that my needs weren't as important," Melanie said. "They were never as urgent as my sister's needs. She was the one who had all the challenges, so whatever she was doing was always more important than whatever I was going through. Invariably any conversation we would have would always go back to my sister."

"In what way?"

"In all ways, even about things that weren't related to her disabilities. For example, I remember Hannah and I went out to an event in the city, a parade or something. We started chatting with one of the policemen and he seemed to take a shining to me. I came home and said to Mom, 'Oh my gosh, I chatted with this really cute police officer.' Her first response was to ask: 'How was your sister? Was she okay with that? Did she feel jealous? Did she feel threatened?' And I just looked at her and thought to myself: 'Really? I'm trying to share something with you that was fun and you automatically ask me how my sister handled it?' Hannah is seven years older. One of the hardest things for me was that I was never the little sister. I was basically the same as an older sister. It was always 'you have to take care of Hannah.'"

I asked Melanie if she ever talked to her mother about her feelings.

"One time, yes. I did try to have a conversation with her."

"How did it go?"

"My mother was a super-woman," Melanie said. "She was someone who really wanted to be all things to all people — a great wife, a great friend, and a great mom. She took a lot of pride in that. Because of that, she had a great deal of difficulty hearing that someone thought that she wasn't living up to those expectations, and that's essentially what I was telling her in the one serious conversation we had about it."

"How did it happen?" I asked.

"I called her and asked her to come meet me for lunch. I was an adult by that time and living on my own. I worked way downtown in the financial district, so I asked her to come meet me there. I did that intentionally because I figured if I made a real appointment with her and had her come all the way downtown, it would seem all the more important. So we were having lunch and I said to her, as gently as I could, 'Mom, I feel like you don't really listen to me. I feel like you're not really available to me.'"

"What was her reaction?"

"She looked at me as if I had said the moon was made of blue cheese. She couldn't imagine I felt such a thing. She said, 'What are you talking about? I'm always there if you need me.' I could tell that she just couldn't hear what I was saying. I cried and said, 'That's not true.'"

"Did you continue talking about it?" I asked.

"No. Not that day. I dropped it, but I never forgot it. Oh sure, if I was in a crisis or if I was in a really horrible situation, I could go to her, but for every day issues — no. She really wasn't there. After that, I never went back to my mother to express my feelings because she could not hear it. She didn't want to hear it. After she passed away, I talked about it with a lot of her close friends. They all said they took her aside at one time or another to tell her that she needed to be there for me. Her response was always, 'Melanie's fine.' It was almost like I got penalized for not having the same challenges as my sister. It was like my needs weren't real. She would make the time to do things with Hannah. I remember once she went to a Broadway show with Hannah — she and I never did that alone together."

"Where was your father in all this?" I asked. "Was he like that too?"

"No. Not at all. My father was very supportive and understanding because he was going through it too. He was not Hannah's biological father. Both of my parents had previous marriages. But he adopted Hannah, so for all intents and purposes, she was his daughter."

"And your mother's focus on Hannah came at the expense of the others in the family."

"At times, yes. My mother was so focused and so consumed by her anxiety over Hannah that there often wasn't that much space for the rest of us. It was exhausting. Every time we thought there was going to be a light at the end of the tunnel it never seemed to come because, unfortunately, Hannah has had a lot of sorrow in her life that is unrelated to her learning disabilities. Even so, it always seemed like everything was yet another reason for Mom to keep holding onto her very tightly."

I asked Melanie when she first became aware that Hannah might have a disability.

"There are two things," she said. "I remember Mom spending a lot of time with Hannah on her homework — much more time than she spent with me. I didn't need help with my homework. The other thing is that I would sometimes do Hannah's English homework for her and I remember thinking it was kind of unusual that I was doing my older sister's homework."

"No one ever told you what was going on with your sister?"

"No, never."

"How old were you at this time?"

"I would have been about nine or ten," she said, "but I don't remember any conversation where anyone told me about Hannah's disabilities."

"Do you think it would have helped if someone had sat down with you and explained the situation?"

Melanie paused for a moment, thinking. "That's a hard question to answer."

"Why?"

"Because I don't know that it would have changed the ultimate outcome, which was that Mom wasn't available. I knew my sister had challenges, even if there wasn't a formal conversation. I understood that. It wasn't something that was difficult to figure out, given what was taking place. It was more an issue of whether or not there was enough room on Mom's plate to be a full-time mother to me too. There was a constant refrain of, 'someday when you're a mother, you'll understand,' or 'no one understands how I feel and how I suffer.'"

"That was your mother's explanation?"

"Oh yes, absolutely. She genuinely felt that way, with both me and my father. She felt that we didn't understand what she was going through. And of course, to a certain extent that's true. But it evolved into a Her vs. Us scenario. She felt we couldn't possibly understand why she had to protect Hannah so ferociously and it ended up creating a space between us."

I could sense Melanie's emotions rising to the surface, still powerful after all these years. "You still have strong feelings about this."

"I do," Melanie said. "Especially since my mother is not here. It is a wound that never goes away. Part of that wound comes from knowing that I didn't revisit that conversation downtown. I felt like it fell on deaf ears. I said to myself, 'I tried, she didn't hear me, I'm not doing it again.' And then she got sick so I was never able to have that conversation."

I sat back, remembering Jennifer's smile when praising Melanie and her pride in her daughter's success. "She talked to me a lot about you," I said. "She was so proud when you graduated from Columbia. She was very, very proud of you."

"It's weird because Dad said that to me too after she died, about how proud she was of me."

"Do you believe it?"

"I do," Melanie said. "I don't doubt that she loved me and that she was proud of me, but like I said, I almost feel I got penalized for being the one she didn't have to worry about."

I asked if she ever began to resent Hannah and she reared back with a laugh and said, "Oh, absolutely! There was a long period when I really resented her. And then I reached a place where I realized that I couldn't put that entirely on her and that Mom made choices about how she was going to handle it."

"When did that resentment reach its peak? At what age?"

"In my early twenties is when it really started to bother me at a visceral level. I had just done my junior year in London and I came home and went through what they call Re-entry Shock. I was not happy to be home. It was terrible. I was not fun to be around when I came back. I had received a little pamphlet from my home college that addressed the problem of Re-entry Shock. It described all the things I was going through. I remember giving it to Mom to get her to understand that my feelings were real and that I was going through a difficult transition, but she didn't want to hear any of it. Her response was, 'You had a great year in London. What are you complaining about?' And again, whatever Hannah was going through at that time was so much more important than anything I was going through. I felt like it didn't really matter that I was going through anything. Mom's attitude was, 'You can handle it. Hannah's the one who needs my attention.' That was true to a certain extent, but I still needed my mother."

"You said the word 'visceral' a moment ago. Have you reached a place where you realize you still feel these things, but understand and accept them on a more intellectual level?"

"It depends on when you ask me," she said with another laugh. "I know Mom did the best that she could. I know she loved us both. So yes, intellectually, I do understand that. But at that emotional, visceral level, it's difficult — especially because she died so young. She was fifty-seven. Because of that, I feel doubly short-changed. Had she lived maybe it would be a different story."

"You could have eventually reached some understanding with each other."

"It is a question that will never be answered for me. It is the wound I will have to live with the rest of my life."

I asked Melanie if her mother ever did anything special with her, a trip alone, for example.

"No," she said. "Sometimes I would suggest that to her, but she would say, 'How can I go on a trip? You know how busy I am looking after your father and your sister.' There was always an excuse. And so yes, going back to your earlier question, I did resent my sister because she had a lot of quality alone time with my mother."

"But in the long run, it really hasn't helped Hannah," I said. "I think it made her feel so dependent on her mother that when she got married, she had no idea what she was doing. She never grew up."

"That's right," Melanie said. "And then it became this insidious thing where my father took over the role my mother had. Before she died, Mom said, 'Promise me you'll do exactly what I've been doing and take care of Hannah when I'm not here.' Who could say no to that? So he did the same thing, he coddled her, although he did it a little more resentfully. That affected my relationship with him too, but in a different way. We would spend time together and he would just vent. He was overwhelmed with having to deal with the situation, and I thought, 'Oh my God, here we go all over again. I can't even have a conversation with my father because it's all about how Hannah is driving him crazy.'

"But in that case it was because Hannah was driving him crazy. It wasn't because he felt so sorry for her."

"No, not at all."

"It sounds like a situation bound to cause resentments on all sides," I said.

"That's right, and I will never really be able to escape the feeling that things weren't fair. I have no way to change that now."

"It would be nice if someone like your mother could read this and reevaluate her own situation. Most parents honestly believe they are being fair." I asked Melanie why she thought her mother was so anxious about her sister. Not every mother is so hyper-focused on the child with special needs.

"Hannah's learning disabilities were diagnosed a little late," she said. "I remember hearing that my mother had really come down hard on my sister when she was younger and not bringing in the grades. She accused her of not trying hard enough and being lazy. I think she was haunted by that. I think she felt she had to make up for the past."

"How is your relationship with your sister now?"

"We have our ups and downs, like most siblings," Melanie said. "Sometimes I wish I could just get everything off my chest with her. I remember one time many years ago she just looked at me and said, 'Why do you hate me so much?' At that moment I felt really bad that she felt that way. At the same time I wanted to say, 'Oh, you noticed?' That would have been the opportunity to confront the issue, but I didn't. Instead I said, "I don't hate you," and I swept it under the rug."

"She needs you," I suggested, but Melanie seemed doubtful. "Yeah, I guess," she said. "But although Hannah is vulnerable, I feel that sometimes people overestimate how vulnerable she is. She's a lot stronger than people think. That's another thing that irks me. Mom was so worried about her. She would say, 'Hannah is going to fall apart when I'm not here' — but Hannah went ice-skating the day of Mom's funeral! I was in a ball on the floor, but Hannah went on."

"Do you think things would have been easier for you if Hannah had been more obviously disabled?

"Probably. To me there was always a disconnect between what she had and the way Mom treated her. I didn't see her as being the helpless victim in the same way Mom did."

"That is common with LD," I said. "I think you had a greater challenge because your sister's LD isn't obvious, which in turn, would give you a real sense of injustice and inequality."

"That's exactly the way I felt. The word inequality is a good one because I really did feel that it didn't matter how much I accomplished. If I did something wrong I would get punished for it, while Hannah could do something much worse and not get punished at all. If I said anything about it, my mother's reaction was, 'Well, Hannah is different. Hannah has problems. We have to make allowances for her.' There were completely different sets of rules. I really did feel that it was unfair and not equal."

"It sounds to me like your mother had a bit of an obsession over Hannah," I said. "That can become a real problem for some parents. The focus on the one child takes precedence over everything else. In their mind they are doing the right thing — but there is no balance. And obviously this has had long-lasting effects. If you had one thing to say to those parents, what would it be?"

"The first thing I would say is '*Listen*.' When the child who doesn't have the challenge finds the courage to say, 'I'm not getting what I need,' you need to pay attention to..." Melanie suddenly broke down. She paused for a moment to wipe her eyes and then continued through her tears. "You need pay attention to that. As hard as it is to hear, you need to pay attention. It takes a lot of courage to have that conversation when you're the one who feels you're not getting what you need. I loved my mother, I respected her, I looked up to her; and she took great pride in being there for everyone, so it was very difficult to say anything to her. I remember scheduling that lunch and being really nervous about it. And then to sit down with her and have her look at me as if what I was saying was completely wrong." Melanie wiped her eyes again and then straightened in her chair, recovering. "That was very hard," she said. "It basically shut me down because it took so much to say that to her and she couldn't hear it. So I think that's really important. To listen. And also to try to say to yourself, 'Just because the other child doesn't have the same challenges doesn't mean their problems and their feelings aren't as important and don't need attention.' I'm not saying to give the same amount of time to the non-disabled child as you do the child with special needs, but to guard against automatically turning everything back to the disabled child when having a conversation with your other children. In that moment, try to focus on the child you are talking to. I always felt, no matter what I talked to my mother about, it always went back to Hannah. Always."

"One of the things that strikes me when you talk about your mother is how close to the surface this is for you, and how the feelings are still so strong."

"They are," Melanie said. "It will be thirteen years in a couple of weeks that Mom has been gone. As I said, it's still a wound that will never go away. It consists of two things: the frustration that she couldn't hear what I needed to tell her and the time I wasted being resentful instead of taking her aside again and making it a priority. I just assumed it would happen eventually. When she got sick, I told myself 'when she gets better I'll bring it up again.'

"What might have been," I said wistfully.

"Yes, what might have been. And that leads to the other piece of advice I have, and this is for older children who are going through it now. Make your feelings a priority. Don't let your concerns fall on deaf ears. If you're not heard the first time, go back a second and a third time. You don't ever want to sit back and say, 'Wow, I expected her to be a mind reader.' It was hard for her to hear that she was letting me down. My mother and I were both into collecting Barbie dolls. I came home one day and for no reason, she had bought me a beautiful Barbie and left it on my bed with a card that said something sweet about what a great daughter I was. I remember looking at that card and being completely unmoved. I just thought, 'Well, so what? A card's easy. You're not there when I need to talk to you.' And again, that was a missed opportunity because I could have gone in there and said that to her. I could have thanked her for the Barbie and then told her what I really needed, but I didn't do that. So that's my advice if you're a child going through it and feeling that way. Make it a priority. Don't give up just because it doesn't work the first time you try. It's important to avoid falling into the trap of thinking you have all the time in the world because sometimes you don't get that time. You never know what the future will bring."

"IF THEY HAD ONLY TOLD ME"

I met a gentleman in the course of writing this book who, like Melanie in the previous chapter, admitted to harboring resentments against his parents and the attention paid to his younger brother, though his is far from an active resentment. Rather than interview him, I asked him to write his thoughts down. This is what he came up with.

I have a younger brother with learning disabilities and was asked if I felt any lingering resentment toward my brother or my parents over the inequality of attention we received. Without thinking, I said no. My brother was diagnosed with learning disabilities when he was in junior high (though I was never told this until much later). I was two years older. We had no other siblings. So I said "No" when asked if I had resentments, and I meant it. I didn't and don't, but then I thought about it and realized, "you know what? I *do!*"

This is the situation: I do not have any sort of active, overt resentment against my brother or my parents. I never did have it, even back when it was all happening, because I absolutely knew without question that he needed the help. He was on a path to destruction, even at that young age. He had already gotten in trouble with the law and began to experiment with substance abuse. He started to hang out with the wrong crowd. There was no way he was going to straighten himself out on his own, so my father sacrificed a great deal to send my brother to a very strict private school while I continued on in the much less prestigious public school.

I was a good student and got good grades, and you know how it is in high school — I was happy being with my friends and would have rebelled at the thought of going to my younger brother's private school. Only later did I realize what a step-up that would have been for me and how much better prepared I would have been for college.

My parents also focused on my brother's activities and interests much more intensely than on mine. There was a token nod in my direction, but it was clear that most of their energies were directed toward ensuring my brother didn't feel left out. Again — all that attention was probably necessary and did a world of good. My brother's self-esteem remained healthy and his LD did not prevent him from achieving success later in life.

So all in all, things worked out in our family. If I could change only one thing, I would not want it to be that my parents spent more time with me, or praised me more often, or attended more of my basketball games. It would be this: I wish they would have *only once* told me the reason for the imbalance in attention. Seriously — one time would have been enough. I am reasonably intelligent and I would have immediately grasped the truth of their statement. A one-minute explanation would have eliminated years of self-questioning.

That would be my advice to other parents. Even if you think your children without LD understand why you're doing the things you do, take a break and sit down with them and tell them exactly why you're doing it. Don't assume they know, and even if they do know, don't assume they don't need to hear it from you.

It's a simple thing, but it will last a lifetime.

"IF SHE'S SO SPECIAL, WHAT AM I?"

Sarah and Kim

Sarah was thirty-three years old and married with two children when I spoke with her. I started by asking her when she first became aware of her sister Kim's learning challenges.

"I can pinpoint it exactly," she said. "I was in first grade and she was in third grade. We were in the back seat of the car doing times tables. My aunt was in the front seat and she was asking Kim, 'What's three times three?' I was two years younger than Kim, so I obviously didn't know the answer. But they were doing multiplication in Kim's class and she didn't know the answer either. She kept saying 'two', and our aunt kept saying, 'no, it's not.' After about the fifth time I said, 'Kim, it's nine. She gave you the answer five times! It's *nine*." I remember thinking, 'wait…I'm understanding something that Kim who is my older sister can't understand.'"

"How did that make you feel?"

"I remember being confused. At that age, a child has no perception of 'the big picture'. Everything for a child is here and now and immediate and I think you need to get a little older before you really understand what is happening."

"Sometimes siblings can't understand learning disabilities," I said, "especially when it's the older brother or sister who has LD. Did you see other things?"

"More than anything, I saw emotional situations."

"Related to her learning disabilities?" I asked. Emotional problems are not something that we automatically see in individuals with LD.

"I don't know if they were related, but they were there," Sarah said. "There were two standards for how we behaved emotionally in our house. My younger brother Jeff and I were brought up with one set of standards and Kim was brought up with another. She was allowed to get away with things that we were not. She would cry and talk back to my mother and father – more to my mother. She could talk back to Mom and say things that Jeff and I would never dream of saying. We knew from an early age that that just wasn't the way you do things, and somehow Kim was allowed to do it. She would get upset and didn't know how to verbalize properly. There were other things too...when she was in the middle grades, she would take my toothbrush, or if I wore a new sweater, the next thing I knew, Kim would be wearing it. And I would go to my mother and tell her she took my brand new sweater, and my mother would say, 'She's different, she's special, just let her wear it.' But I would never have been able to do that to Kim."

"Did you feel a sense of unfairness?"

"Of course! On Saturday, before we could go out and play, we all had to clean our rooms. Kim would take the cover and just throw it over the bed while Jeff and I would work for thirty minutes organizing our shoes and our closets. Kim could go right out and play while we had to stay there. We'd say, 'Mom, how come Kim can go out and play?' and the answer would always be, 'Because Kim is special.' Over and over, those were the words I heard: 'Kim is special.' Well, what does that make me? *Not* special? I thought I was doing everything right, but Kim was the one who was called special. And in my particular situation, I had a younger brother who was the apple of my father's eye, and my mother was so focused on Kim that I think I have a classic case of Middle Child Syndrome. Honestly, it wasn't until Kim left for school when a lot of people said I finally came out of my shell and got to talk and speak. I wasn't scared anymore."

"Scared?" I asked, thinking that was a peculiar reaction to a having a sibling with LD. "What scared you?"

"I kept thinking I was doing something wrong. I really did. I thought there was something wrong with me."

"Did your mother ever sit down and tell you exactly what was going on?"

"I knew enough to know that she was hurting, so I didn't want to bring it up. She would say 'Kim is special' or 'Kim is not like you', but the truth is, she was still trying to figure it out herself. She didn't know what was wrong with Kim either. But as a child your world is black and white. You want to know what is wrong and my parents did not have definitive answers. My mother would tell me Kim was different and had a different way of learning. She was trying so hard to avoid saying Kim was less than anyone else. But that meant other things had to be put on hold."

"What do you mean by that?" I asked.

"For example, when I turned sixteen, I wanted to get my driver's license. Everyone does when they turn sixteen. Mom didn't want me to get my driver's license because she was afraid it would hurt Kim's feelings. I think that might have been the first time I put my foot down. I said, 'I'm not going to give up my driver's license because of Kim's feelings'. I had put everything on hold for so long already because of Kim. At the same time, looking back at it now as a mother, I don't know what I would have done differently and I now believe my mother did the best she could. I don't think there is any way to please two or three people in that situation, but when you're that age, it's very hard to grasp 'She is special and you're not.'"

I said that I was glad she brought up this story as I think it nicely illustrates the problem many siblings face. By trying to shield the feelings of one child, parents can't help but hurt the other. No mother actively ignores one of her children but certainly the focus on the child with LD makes it appear that way.

Sarah agreed. "In our house it was a matter of 'let's have family meetings about how to deal with Kim'. Once when Kim had problems with me, I was the one who was sent to see a counselor. So I went to a counselor to talk about Kim. Our entire family went to a counselor to talk about Kim. Everything centered around Kim. At the same time, these days Kim truly is my best friend. We talk constantly on the telephone. She calls every single night to check up on the kids. I appreciate her so much, so thankfully I don't have a resentment that is going to last the rest of my life."

"I find that's the case with many adult siblings," I said. "Once they are mature enough to see and understand their brother or sister's problem, they become much more accepting of their own past. Of course, some adults never really come to terms with it and carry their resentments long into adulthood. When they are young, they often have a sense that they can't do anything to get their parents to pay attention to them. They try so hard, they achieve more, they strive more, but they still never get the recognition."

"That's true," Sarah said. "My husband told me recently that I'm still clamoring for my parents' attention. I sometimes feel that all my life was spent jumping up and down and shouting, 'Hello! I'm here!' Every time I did something that I thought warranted a 'that is great' response, I didn't get it. They didn't want to overdo the 'that is great!' stuff with me. They would say, 'That is good,' and then turn to Kim and say, "Oh Kim, you took two steps, that is awesome, that is *great!*"

I asked Sarah what she would say to a mother who is going through this with her own children.

"I thought about this a lot because I don't know how my mother could have changed much of what she did. For one thing I would never tell one child he or she is special, especially if there is any chance of making another child feel that he or she is not special. I would also sit down and talk to the sibling one on one. It wasn't until Kim left home and my mother and I started traveling together and spending time alone together that I realized that I actually *was* special in her eyes, but in a way that was different from Kim. So I would definitely recommend spending some one on one time with the other children and let them know that they are really as important as the child with LD, even if you think they already know that. Another thing that's important is to be honest about the situation. For example you could say, 'I am so thrilled with your straight A's and I am so proud of you for your accomplishments, and I realize I don't tell you that enough."

"What would you say Kim has brought to your life as the sibling of someone with LD?" I asked.

"I can answer that two ways," Sarah said. "As a child she brought the realization that things aren't always as easy as they may appear from the outside. There were some hard times that I didn't understand. It was complicated and it was stressful and I didn't like the way I felt about her. I didn't want her around. I didn't want her in my room because every time she was around she was mean to me or to my friends. I now realize that she was jealous of me just living my life, but at the time I wanted to play over at everyone else's house because

I didn't want Kim around. Every time she came around I got embarrassed. I went through that whole embarrassment stage. I walked around embarrassed for about four years."

"And then you felt guilty about being embarrassed," I said.

"Yes. I thought she was always slightly off and weird and I didn't know why because no one really explained it to me. As far as I was concerned, she was weird, she didn't act her age, she hit me in public; and I remember shutting down and not talking about it. I also remember that we were so close in age that people would sometimes call me Kim, and I would say, 'Uh-uh, I'm *not* Kim!'"

"How old were you in this period?"

"Probably from eleven to fifteen. So that's the first way I can talk about what Kim brought to my life. At that age it seemed she brought only difficulties and embarrassment. The second way I can talk about what she has brought to my life is as an adult. She brings clarity to everything I do. Things are clear-cut with her. There isn't a lot of internal debate. She gets to the heart of things very quickly, so if you look at life from Kim's perspective, it can simplify things."

"Do you think she's given you a heightened sense of compassion for others?"

"Oh yes, absolutely. I don't think people who do not have a sibling or family member with a disability have the same sort of patience or understanding."

"I feel the same," I said. "I believe a person with disabilities brings value to everyone else in the family. It allows you to see that people aren't perfect, and that families aren't perfect."

"Kim was maid of honor in my wedding and I had friends who said it was so sweet of me to include her. My attitude was that it had nothing to do with being sweet or not - she's my sister!"

"Do you remember people saying insensitive things to you about Kim when you were young?"

"Yes. And when I was young I thought, 'wow, that's what people think.' I didn't stand up for her. It wasn't until she went away to a special school that I started getting protective of Kim."

"When she went away were you relieved? Were you upset?"

"I cried, but I think it was mostly the fear of the unknown. We used to share a bathroom, and I remember feeling like I could finally lay out my brush and my toothbrush without worrying about her taking them. So I was also relieved. Every time she came back into town, I would hide things under my bed. I knew if I had a favorite sweater she would take it. Within two or three years, all that changed. When I went to see her at the school and saw her with the other disabled students, I was really proud of her. I remember walking around the school and seeing that she was flourishing there and doing well, and I felt pride for the first time."

"Were there other challenges you faced as the sister of someone with LD?" I asked.

"They all come down to the feeling of being excluded, or that your feelings on the matter do not really count. For instance, everyone always asks Mom how she dealt with everything or they'll ask her if it was hard on her. I *know* it was hard on her, but very rarely does anyone ask if it was hard on me too."

"The mothers can contribute to that as well," I said. "Sometimes we mothers think we are the only ones truly affected by it. We get used to the idea that we are the only one involved, and we become obsessed because we have to be. But then you get these additional burdens down the road. You learn that you didn't pay enough attention to your other children, and you can start to beat yourself up for being too much of an advocate. It's very difficult, but that's the reality of the situation. Too many mothers get these things thrown on top of them. Even when you think the problems are almost over, another one comes along. That's why you see women involved for so long in some of the learning disabilities organizations. They are still obsessed with a child who has long been an adult! For some of these mothers, there seems to be nothing she can do to heal the pain. Even so, I believe most mothers would say of her child with LD – of *all* her children – that they are a blessing, even with all the difficulties. And the disability has been a blessing in its own way because it has made others in the family more human, more compassionate and more understanding of people."

"I completely agree," said Sarah. "My sister made me who I am."

Siblings
A Professional View

"LD is not who you are –
it's what you have.'

A MATTER OF BALANCE

~ Dr. Sheldon Horowitz ~

*W*hen I was Chairman of the National Center for Learning Disabilities I was lucky enough to work with Dr. Sheldon Horowitz, Director of Professional Services. Dr. Horowitz is our resident expert on all things related to the well-known challenges of learning disabilities, but he is equally at home discussing the more personal, family-centered problems as well.

Here is his take on sibling issues:

When talking about siblings, it is important to frame the discussion around the dynamics of the family. Every family operates in its own unique way and is influenced by an ever-changing mix of parenting styles, personalities, outside influences and emotions. Each person in the family contributes to the family dynamic in ways that reflect their needs and desires, which are greatly influenced by where they are in their life journey. Think about the stereotypical family: parents are often expected to have "all the answers," older siblings are supposed to "set examples," and younger siblings are "cut some slack." The reality is more complicated, and if you then add a child with learning disabilities into the mix, it can get even more complicated.

If parenting came with a rulebook, it would all be easy, but we all know it doesn't work that way. Things get more complicated when a child is deemed to be vulnerable and in need of closer supervision and a more intensive level of a parent's support. The family balance is upset. The roles of parents and siblings are shifted and the flow of family living is sprinkled (or flooded!) with anxiety and worry. The emotional wiring of the family begins to fray and a tension between dependence and independence takes hold. Roles get redefined. Attention gets paid in ways that don't always seem fair and each member of the family is faced with having to decide what they really need and what they are willing to give up for the well-being of the others. There is no question that children who are perceived to be more in need of special help often get more attention than others, or a different kind of attention than others. Inadvertently, this can shape the roles of family members and very often, siblings are left to make sense of this imbalance on their own.

Sibling issues often challenge the comfort level of the parents and how they feel about having a child with special needs, or the extent to which they see themselves as caretaking and nurturing in a particular way that may not match with what the child ultimately wants or needs. When you look at it in terms of children with a learning disability, there are some parents who are helicoptering way too much and for way too long. Those children are not, for example, taking the initiative to go up to a teacher to talk about their IEP (Individualized Education Plan) or requesting an accommodation such as getting copies of class notes. At some point, children with LD need to be able to say those things to their teachers – and the sooner the better. This does not mean parents should give up being in close communication with school personnel or remain vigilant about grades, services, supports, and transition planning. They definitely should, so it's a combination of parenting and how that translates into how comfortable the child feels about being part of the solution. You want the child to be able to say, 'What's my role in all this? What's my mom and dad's role? Don't judge me by what I can't do. Judge me by what I *can* do and help me get from point A to point B.'

Now let's circle back to the issue of siblings Let's say the family routine is for everyone to help themselves to cereal in the morning, but your son without LD is encouraged to make his own eggs while his older sister with LD is allowed to use the toaster but is told to stay away from the stove. Why is that? Is it presumed that she is not as coordinated as her younger brother and might turn the burner on too high or forget to turn it off? That might be fine to start, but could quickly translate into learned helplessness or dependency. There is nothing that eats away at someone's self concept like other people saying, 'you can't, you shouldn't, you won't, you don't'. This is very important. If the parents are confident with their goals for all their children, and if they set and maintain high expectations for their disabled child's outcomes (even when they don't know what those outcomes will be), the better it will be for the family as a whole.

Some parents let these things go. They don't address problems between siblings. These problems should be talked about. The conversation should happen at the kitchen table with the spouse, with the other children, and with the special needs child. It should happen with everyone, even with grandparents, nieces and nephews and baby-sitters. This is not something you hide and allow to fester until it becomes emotionally explosive. It is something you need to work with in the open because its part of the reality of having a child with a learning disability.

When LD Rules the Roost

We sometimes hear about situations where the child with LD ends up ruling the household. Some mothers believe it's easier to avoid things as they come up and instead, allow the child's moods and whims to dictate for the whole family. But no child should be running the household. He or she should be *part* of the household — not running it. There are ways to prevent it from happening. It sounds simple - and I know from my own family as well as families I have worked with that it is not - but the bottom line is this: you need to decide right away who the parent is.

As the parent, you set certain rules. Every household should have rules, whether there are children with LD or not. In my house, some of those rules are 1) no hitting or threatening physical violence. 2) No language that is offensive to anyone else (even if they are not present.) 3) Everyone cleans up after themselves: kitchen, bathroom, bedroom, TV area — no exceptions. I say, 'These rules are non-negotiable. You don't have to like them, you just have to live with them. At whatever point you can afford to move out and live a different lifestyle, I'm happy to visit, but as long as you're here, these are my rules.' Another spoken expectation is that people in the family don't have to agree, but everyone in the family will have a voice and will be treated with respect. No parent or sibling should ever be belittled, tormented or bullied by anyone else in the family. Families deal with all kinds of challenges: parents out of work or underemployed; infirm relatives who require extensive care; substance abuse, anxiety, depression and other mental health disorders; and then there are the less traumatic but still important hurdles like juggling schedules, chasing monsters out from under the beds, tooth fairy visits, birthday celebrations and so on. All of these family issues impact children with LD as well as their siblings, and trying to make sure that everyone is included and valued can seem like an overwhelming feat. But it's the only way to ensure that the family functions well as a cohesive unit. It's the only way to ensure that no one feels left out, overlooked or put upon, and that the family can function as the safe haven and safety net that it is truly intended to be.

Having said that, things are not always so clear when it comes to learning disabilities. Some families are held hostage to the child's moods. In other families, the mother simply says, 'Well, I don't put up with that.' So much depends on parenting style. If the child is out of control and needs some therapeutic or pharmacological intervention, then you as a family need to work together to make sure that child knows how to fit into the family and into society. If you took that child into a restaurant, he wouldn't be throwing things around and running into the kitchen and breaking dishes. He might make noise at the table, but he wouldn't be so completely dysfunctional and controlling. The reality is this: if he can hold it together at the restaurant, he can hold it together in the house. You have to set up the rules. A child holding the entire family hostage to his or her moods is not acceptable, and more often than not, big changes can be realized by setting clear expectations and modeling the behaviors you want to see in your child. Part of what makes it particularly difficult for families of children with LD is that, because schoolwork is so hard for them, they need more attention and more time just to get that schoolwork done. It's harder for them to get organized. They need help finding and organizing their papers.

They need help checking over their spelling and proofreading their written work. They need help setting up assignments and a lot of feedback during the process of completing their work. This can become overwhelming and more than a little stressful for the parent.

A Matter of Balance

It can be stressful for the sibling too. When looking at the amount of time that is devoted to the child with LD, a sibling can wonder, 'Why does mommy love him more?' or 'Why is he getting all the attention? Maybe if I stop doing well in school, I'll get some of that attention too.' Part of the challenge for parents and for families is to figure out who needs what by way of attention and real time on tasks. And the issue of fairness in terms of parental attention sometimes seems to favor the disabled child. But that's not always true. The child with LD may feel they are getting the short end of the stick when it comes to parental attention; for instance it may be that the child with LD has to give up going to Boy Scout meetings or taking tennis lessons because they have to spend so much time on school work. Sure, that child is getting extra attention, but I'm sure he or she doesn't see it that way — it's much more fun to have a tennis lesson than focus on school work."

It's all a matter of balance, which isn't always easy, and the balance needs to be a good fit for each child. There should not be a consuming over-importance placed on the needs of one child versus another.

The Daily Check-in

We sometimes hear from older siblings that they feel they are left to fend for themselves. To avoid this feeling of detachment, a parent should initiate a conversation that sounds like this: 'I know I'm spending a lot of time with your brother on schoolwork. It's really hard for him and it's really hard for me. But let's you and I check-in every day so I know how you are doing.' Have that conversation. Let that non-disabled sibling know that he has your attention too. If it needs to be calendared differently or if another person has to come in to help, fine. But make it happen. Just remember that the amount and quality of time and feedback that a non-disabled learner needs will be very different from what the disabled child needs.

That daily check-in with the non-disabled children would solve so many problems.

The Importance of "Soft Skills"

Another thing that is really difficult for children with LD is this: when they're in school, they're being taught math and reading and writing and when they're home, they're doing homework involving math and reading and writing. But there is a disconnect between all that stuff and the skills they need when they go outside on the playground, or for older children, when they're on a job, or training for a job, or baby-sitting….and the things they don't get taught are the very things that can cause trouble between a child and a parent and siblings. They don't develop those people skills. I'll call them 'soft skills.' They can also be thought of as social skills.

They are things you can practice with your child with LD. For example, you go to the supermarket with that child. You want to get three lamb chops and a half a pound of coleslaw. Your child isn't particularly good at math and doesn't remember what coleslaw looks like, and he then has to remember the size or to read the numbers or how to talk to the butcher. Instead of saying, 'watch me do it' or 'come with me,' you should send him up to the counter and let him do it. Let him practice it. Be there with him. You can always make it better if he doesn't get it right. You can practice ahead of time what he's going to ask for. But let him do it. Then ask him how he felt or what he was worried about. Give him that sense of accomplishment, that sense of power, that sense of positive engagement, which then translates in school into the ability to ask the teacher 'can you help me with this?' or 'I didn't get that the first time, could you repeat it?' It's the same with bringing things to the laundry mat or ordering a pizza on the phone or making change – those kinds of things build competency and confidence. You can help a child develop the social skills at the kitchen table, which they can then translate into an ability to talk to people at school or on the job. It's so important for those kids.

You wouldn't think twice about giving your non-LD child a ten dollar bill to go out for a loaf of bread and some milk. With the kid with LD, you might think twice. Why is that? Because you think they might come back with the wrong change, or pick the wrong thing, but those are things he's going to need to get through life. Give him those responsibilities. If you don't, what is the non-disabled sibling going to think? They'll think, "Why do I have to do it all the time? Because Mom is afraid or Dad is concerned that my brother might not get it right?" That's not a good reason. If it's age appropriate and it's something you feel he should be able to do or should be able to grow into doing – remember this: his siblings are watching and they are probably thinking the same thing. Send them out together once in a while. Give the child with LD the list or the money and tell that child, "You are in charge, but your brother will be there if you need him."

"Special"

Some parents are reluctant to talk about or use the words 'learning disability' with siblings and other family members. When that happens, the non-disabled siblings only see the special treatment and don't understand why it's happening. They aren't told the specifics of the problem and are likely to make assumptions about it that are not true. They are only told 'because he's special.'

Parents should talk to the siblings about the learning disabilities as soon as they can. Having said that, it's important to realize that identifying a learning disability involves a discovery process, during which it is important to protect the feelings of everyone involved. As an example of what I mean, let's say a child who has been getting failing grades in spelling and reading is found to have a learning disability. After the diagnosis, a plan is made to improve skills and accelerate learning. The thing *not* to do is to walk into the kitchen where the whole family is gathered and hold up the diagnosis with a fanfare and announce 'this is the reason he was failing!' What you do want to do is say something like this, and only to the child with LD: 'Remember how hard spelling was for you? We all know how difficult it is because we can't read the notes you write to us on the refrigerator. Well, guess what. We know why that's happening now. It has nothing to do with how smart you are. It has everything to do with how your brain is processing information. We still need you to try to write the notes on the refrigerator more legibly, but I bet that will also get better over time. We're here to help if we can. Everyone knows you're smart, and now we know how to help you process information and show off what you know.'

The message should always be "LD is not who you *are*. It's what you *have*."

In some cases, children are not given a firm diagnosis right away so parents do not have a definitive answer to the question of what is going on. Sometimes parents will withhold all information, even when the child with disabilities engages in behaviors his or her siblings find annoying. But to not acknowledge that *something* is going on, even when it isn't clear what it is, can lead to problems. So if a parent knows there is something about their child that is driving the siblings crazy or is problematic outside of the family, this provides an opportunity for the *family* to help. Siblings can play a huge and important role with this. Let's say the child with LD also has features of Asperger's Syndrome, or has a co-occurring problem with attention or language issues that result in awkward social skills. A sibling can provide feedback in ways that are helpful and not hurtful. "You're standing too close," or "That's not a joke you should be retelling with people who don't know you well," can help the child with LD avoid embarrassment. It provides feedback about social cues that are essential to healthy friendships. They can even practice these behaviors at home (often accompanied by hearty laughter). The alternative is allowing yourself to be annoyed or angered and responding with "Don't you get it? That's not funny!" or "Get out of my face!" — and that sort of response is not helpful.

Sometimes parents or siblings allow themselves to assume a role as a martyr, willingly taking the abuse in order to keep peace in the house. This is why we have therapy. If the sibling without LD is angry and the way she takes it out is scapegoating and targeting the mother or the LD sibling, then that is something she needs to work out because the world is not just about her. It is about her in the context of other people with whom she lives. When she moves out, when she goes off to college or she goes into the workplace, is she going to come home and say, 'My life is ruined because I have the two of you to deal with?' No. During the adolescent years, when many of these types of feelings begin to take shape, parents should encourage siblings to focus on what they need to be successful and independent of the family. One angry teenager was stopped in her tracks when her parents said, "If it's so unpleasant to spend so much time here with us, get a hobby or a job. Spend more high-quality time with friends. Or maybe there is something you can do to help your brother and take some of the pressure off of us. Whatever you decide, stop complaining and be more pleasant."

Some children, especially teenagers, are embarrassed by their sibling with LD and that is partly because learning disabilities are in some ways very different from other kinds of disabilities. This is a generalization, of course, but when you interact with a person who has an intellectual impairment or what we used to call mental retardation, there is no question that there are certain things they cannot do for themselves. They think in a much less robust, intellectual way. They're much more dependent. They cannot possibly use the same kind of judgment as most people. They're not engaging on the same level intellectually, socially, or emotionally as others. We can see that and know that about them rather quickly.

But you take someone with LD or ADHD or a combination of the two, or whose social skills deficits are more pronounced, then things can be different. There are often few if any obvious clues about specific areas of struggle. And again, this is a generalization, but even if there are no obvious clues, those disorders may announce that *something* is going on because this person can be physically or socially unpleasant to deal with. They are annoying. They get too close. They tell the same jokes all the time. Their clothes are not buttoned properly. They walk up to someone they barely know and assume they are friends, or they misread social cues. Those sorts of behaviors do not presume the person isn't intellectual or isn't smart or doesn't have good cognitive ability, but they're in your face in a way that is so much less acceptable and it pushes your buttons. It's this 'hidden' nature of LD that is often the hardest part of the disorder. We will say, "He knows so much about current events – why can't he read aloud from the text book without making mistakes?" or "She is so fabulous at math – why can't she get good grades on her tests?" These types of comments are commonly heard in schools and at home until a learning disability is identified."

Children may live together but that does not mean they understand the ways that each other think and need to be taught. In the protective cocoon of the family dynamic, it is helpful for parents and non-disabled siblings to have a conversation about LD and what it is and is not. Questions and comments that inevitably come up include: "Does it make you wonder where this came from? Is there something we could do differently? Is this something that you might also get?" Parents shouldn't shy away from getting tangled up in the details of "he gets more time" or "she's not trying hard enough." These are hard conversations to have, but ideal opportunities to share with and learn from your children.

This can apply to *every* family because every family has this situation with siblings, whether or not there is a child with LD. "You have this, I want that, why did he get this and I didn't?" – that sort of thing. Every family sets up their own rules and deals with situations like that, but it doesn't mean you can't have that conversation. In the healthiest of families, parents are always listening to their children and learning from them. At the same time, children are always listening to and learning from their parents, and hopefully from their siblings; and nobody is more important than anybody else.

Here is a good rule to follow when it comes to this issue: if you, as a parent of a child with LD, have not thought about the impact of that LD on your non-disabled children, then that alone should be a clue that you need to do something. It could simply be a check-in. It could simply be preventive maintenance, sort of like a regularly scheduled oil-change in your car.

You could start by acknowledging there might be an issue. Some kids know how to compartmentalize these things so it doesn't affect them so much. Others may intellectualize it on one level, but do not deal with it so well on an emotional level. Is resentment normal? Sure. Is envy, jealousy and sibling rivalry normal? Absolutely. But we're not talking about the occasional, 'He got a green one and I got a blue one, and green is my favorite color,' or 'Your birthday present cost more than mine.' We're talking something that is felt every single day and especially during the school days each year. Learning disabilities are challenges that don't disappear over time. They are with a person every day, 365 days a year. This needs to be part of the conversation as a family.

The last thought I'd like to share about siblings has to do with the adolescent years. In the best of circumstances, adolescence is a time of enormous change, so parents should be informed, be prepared, and expect the unexpected. Physical, neurobiological and hormonal changes are taking place, and with maturity comes testing the waters and behavioral fireworks (potentially dangerous if not monitored carefully, powerful and beautiful to watch, and memorable, even defining, for years to come). The thinking parts and the feeling parts of the brain are maturing and making connections, all at the same time Teenagers are beginning to look past their parents and outside to the larger community. It's a wild, emotional period. So even if parents do everything perfectly during those middle school/high school years, their adolescent children are going to experience a roller coaster of feelings; about their past; about their siblings and families; about their future. That is why the conversation about siblings is really important. How they feel about themselves is shaped by the important people in their life. The decisions they make about risk-taking such as experimenting with drugs, skipping school, or engaging in promiscuous sexual behavior can be fed by feelings of insecurity and resentment. As important as social pressure can be, some maladaptive behaviors are ways for teens to claim the center of attention they feel was denied to them at home. They may resort to self-medication as an answer to feelings for stress. Safe, open communication between parents and children and especially among siblings can set the stage for long-lasting and trusting relationships that result in more than just happy families — it spills over into play, work and society in general.

Husbands and Wives

When Learning Disabilities Cause Tension in the Home

*T*he subtitle of this book is *When Learning Disabilities Cause Tension in the Home,* and though the main focus is sibling issues, I would like to expand this further into the family and examine the challenges faced by husbands and wives when a child (or possibly one of the parents) is diagnosed with a learning disability. I personally did not have to deal with this problem as I was divorced from Allegra's father long before she was diagnosed, but even after knowing of her disability, he took no active role in her life from that day on. This was a double-edged sword for me: I had no one to share the difficulties with or discuss the various worries and fears that arise with LD but I also had no one to resist or challenge the decisions I finally made.

Most couples deal with the ups and downs as they do other challenges: by accepting and handling the difficulties as they arise, and though there may be the occasional argument or bouts of friction, they usually get through it with no major problems. Others (thankfully rare) cannot withstand the upheaval caused by LD, and the marriage falters and can even fall apart. I believe, as do some experts I have spoken with, this usually indicates there were already cracks in the foundation of the marriage and the diagnosis of a child's LD and the subsequent stresses prove too much for the relationship to bear.

In my third book *A Special Mother*, we spoke to a mother named Lisa who had a son named Ryan with learning disabilities. She agreed to talk to me this time about problems in her marriage, especially when Ryan's LD became a source of much of the difficulty. Lisa said, "There were problems from the beginning, right from when Ryan was diagnosed with LD. There was always a distance on my husband's part. He never felt there was a problem, even after we had a firm diagnosis. It always fell to me to be the advocate, the caretaker, the one who communicated with the school, and the one who helped Ryan with his homework. My husband would always say, 'Well, you're good with that stuff.' Yes, I was, but it would have been nice not to have to do it all on my own. Many of our fights were over what was best for Ryan and me being frustrated and feeling resentful that I had to do it all, and then when I made decisions, he would question them and second-guess them all the time. But he would never participate in the decision-making process."

I asked Lisa if her son's LD was a contributing factor in the difficulties between them.

"It definitely was. It was a catalyst of sorts and brought things to a head. When things were easy and there wasn't any stress, it was fine. But after the diagnosis, when the stresses came in, we didn't have a strong enough relationship to work together on those things so we finally ended up getting a divorce."

"It helps immeasurably to have a strong relationship in place when challenges come," I said. "And that goes for *any* challenge, especially those like LD that do not go away and continue to influence the family for years."

"And we didn't have that type of relationship. Our son's LD really contributed to the problems. We argued about everything from getting the initial diagnosis to putting him on medication to getting tutors and advocates. Those things are expensive, and my ex would say we couldn't afford it. But my priorities for Ryan were different. He would try to push me to put Ryan into a trade school when I really wanted him to have a mainstream education. We fought tooth and nail on everything."

"The financial burdens of LD often come up when we're talking about tension between husbands and wives," I said. "It is especially acute when one partner doesn't believe the child needs all those services."

"Right. And we weren't wealthy by any means, but I felt it was important and that Ryan needed those things. Otherwise, we were setting him up for failure his whole life long. My ex-husband had different ideas about that."

"You once told me the stress and tension sent you into depression."

"It did," Lisa said. "My son having LD was overwhelming, and I felt isolated. My ex-husband didn't think anything was wrong. His family and I never saw eye to eye on things, and there were some real issues aside from my son's diagnosis. He was a really, really difficult child. He was very attached to me. He cried all the time. I would want to sit in the back of the car with my son so he wouldn't cry, and my husband would get upset because he wanted me to sit in the front of the car with him. I couldn't leave my son to go food shopping because my husband couldn't deal with him, so I definitely felt overwhelmed and isolated and angry."

These sort of marital issues do not often come up in school meetings. They *do* come up in family therapy sessions all the time (assuming the couple has agreed to go to therapy), but if not, small daily occurrences such as a disagreement about scheduling a doctor's appointment or whether or not the homework is done can snowball into real problems. The sense of isolation and helplessness can become oppressive.

"I absolutely felt I was alone in this," Lisa told me. "I didn't talk about it. No one wants to admit their marriage isn't perfect or their marriage is in trouble. Even without the involvement of a learning disability, that sort of thing is hard enough. Some people view other couples' marital problems as if they are contagious, the same as they do with learning disabilities. Given the divorce rate, we can probably assume their own marriage may not be that strong either. It makes them uncomfortable because it makes them pay attention to what might be wrong in their own lives."

Even an otherwise happy marriage can take a sudden dark and surprising detour when a child is diagnosed with LD. I have met both mothers and fathers who become so obsessed with their child and (usually) the frustrations and injustices meted out by the school system that they can focus on no other thing. Truly – every conversation, every waking moment is taken up with what the school did or didn't do, or what a teacher said, or trying to figure out the best course of action to help their child. Every parent of a special needs child needs to be a committed advocate – I stress that in every speech I give – but when advocacy crowds out all other aspects of life, when all joys and pleasures and moments of contentment fall to the wayside, the time has come to make some changes. Even the child who is the sole focus of attention can be damaged: in the eyes of the parent, that child *becomes* his or her learning disability. Dr. Horowitz warned against this in the previous chapter when he said "LD is what you have and not who you are." For the obsessive, over-the-top parent , their vibrant, unique, individual child with LD becomes the disability. All other aspects of their character and who they are become subsumed in the parent's view of the child as *only* being disabled and nothing else.

We also cannot discount the feelings of rejection felt by a spouse who previously was an equal partner in the relationship but is now relegated to the sidelines by the partner who obsessively focuses on the needs of the child with LD. In this case, the feelings of the aggrieved partner are not much different than those experienced by the sibling without LD who feels he or she is the Forgotten Child.

But again, thankfully, most marriages do not end up on the rocks due to LD. Even so, it is worthwhile to take an inventory once in a while to see where tensions arise and what may cause them. In the following discussions we will look at some of the common problems experienced by couples who have one or more children with LD. One of those problems — homework — gets a chapter of its own as that can be one of the most galling and irritating problems of all. We will also talk with a happily-married couple who not only have a child with LD but the husband has a diagnosed learning disability as well.

Taken together, along with the previous sibling-related discussions, they form a collection of cautionary tales and solutions that we hope will provide the keys to open the traps of misunderstandings and wounded feelings so many of us fall into.

FAMILY MATTERS

~ a discussion with Carol Eagle, Ph.D. ~

*D*r. Carol Eagle is a clinical Psychologist and Clinical **Professor Emerita of Child Psychiatry**, Department of Psychiatry and Behavioral Sciences at the Albert Einstein College of Medicine. I met with Dr. Eagle to talk about family issues as they relate to a child with special needs. Before we began our discussion of learning disabilities and family dynamics, Dr. Eagle asked, "May I add to the word 'disabilities' the word 'difference'? I ask that because I don't feel that any person is truly either 'normal' or 'disabled'. Sometimes children are born 'different'. They don't fit into a niche and they can throw an entire family into a quandary."

I said, "And by this you are saying a child who does not have a diagnosed disability but is simply different can have similar effects on a family?"

"Yes, that's exactly what I'm saying. There are many different ways of learning and we don't appreciate that enough. Some people learn in a very peculiar way. I was consulted years ago by the mother of an autistic boy who was approximately eight years old at that time. The parents had trouble accepting that he was a mathematical genius. And he truly was - he could solve equations that would terrify most of us if we looked at the page. He was asked how he could do that because other children couldn't and he said, 'Oh, I look up in the clouds and I see the answer up there.' So who knows? He now works at a college in the mail room where he handles the mail, so he has a job. It is a job requiring low skills, but it's the most he can do even though he is also a mathematical genius. That is an extreme example. In most cases, it's as if everyone in the family is a brunette and suddenly you have a red-headed child. That child does not have a disability. That child is different."

"The challenge with all these various terms has always been the varying levels of disability or difference," I said. "You can find someone who has a mild difference or someone who is profoundly disabled."

"Yes, of course, and then there are special classes and special this and special that. Let me tell you about another case I worked on once. It was a twelve year old girl. I usually work with children, and I use the parents as a resource to help treat the child. These parents were in the middle of a divorce when the girl started coming to me. Early on in the sessions, we were going to play a game and I asked her to read the instructions to me because I didn't know how to play. She said, 'Oh, I can't do that,' and when I asked her why, she very proudly said, 'Because I'm dyslexic.' My response was to say, 'What's that got to do with it? You can still read it to me.' So she then haltingly read it."

"Perfectly?" I asked.

"No. She had trouble, but her dyslexia wasn't so severe that she couldn't understand the rules she was reading. She had started work with a tutor for remedial reading at that time and I thought she had an interesting twist on things. Instead of saying 'oh poor me, I have dyslexia,' she very proudly said she was dyslexic. That was why I called her on it.'

"She used it to get her way?"

"Sure! She did it so she wouldn't have to work at reading these words. We started making some progress, but then a battle began with the child's father. He had a problem because of all the expenses. She had the reading tutor, a psychotherapist, and so forth; and so I had to have a session with him about this. He insisted that she was not learning disabled. I said that was very interesting since the school, the doctors, her mother and everyone else thought she was, and she had been tested and found to have LD. He still resisted. He said, 'I was like that when I was in school." He then told me that his school years were an unhappy, awful time and finished by saying, 'and look at me today!' He had a very successful career and had done very well. I said, 'yes, but even with all that, it must have been awfully difficult for you. That's what I'm working on with your daughter. She needs support so she doesn't have to go through such difficulties or suffer in terms of her image of herself.' So he backed off and they were able to continue. The daughter ended up having a straight-A record in school."

"And the father accepts it now?" I asked.

"The father says she is very bright and that he always knew she was bright."

"It sounds to me like his ego was getting in the way."

"It is definitely an ego issue," said Dr. Eagle. "The child's mother was very proud of her. I was very proud of her. And she is very proud of herself. That was the real achievement. Instead of using 'I'm dyslexic' as a way to get around things, she is now proud of the fact that she can do the work."

"All the extra help she required can be expensive," I said.

"Yes, but it's also a miracle when you see the combination of therapy and remediation working so well."

I asked Dr. Eagle what she would say if a wife came to her and said that her husband is resistant to accepting their child's LD.

"I would tell her to send him to me," she said. "I would want to talk to him."

"So the advice would be to send the husband to talk to a therapist such as yourself."

"Oh, definitely. He is the father of the child."

"And what would your approach be in this instance?"

"My approach is to first ask him about himself and things like 'What was third grade like for you?' I would look for the kinds of problems he experienced growing up. Maybe he was terrible in sports. Maybe he couldn't carry a tune. Who knows? I would be looking for some weakness, some problem area that he felt caused him some difficulty or suffering, and then relate that to what his child is experiencing now."

"In the case of the twelve year old girl whose parents were divorced, do you think their marital troubles were a result of having a child with a disability and that one parent accepted the situation and the other was in denial or less accepting?"

"It's hard for me to say that was the specific cause of the divorce."

"But these sorts of issues can lead to marital problems."

"Oh, yes, they certainly can! I haven't seen it happen when there's a child with a mild learning disability, but I have definitely seen it when there's a child with autism. I have worked with the parents of autistic children in this very way we're talking about, in terms of accepting that this is not only a different child, but a *very* different child."

"So they come to you because they have a child with autism," I said. "I assume there could be different scenarios. One is that both parents don't accept it. Another is that one accepts it and the other doesn't. Or they accept it at different times. What advice do you have for a couple where the wife is feeling completely overwhelmed by the demands of the child with disabilities and no longer has any time for her husband?"

"I worked with a couple who had a severely autistic girl. The husband's complaint was that the wife thought more about the child than she did him. 'Oh, that's not true,' she said. 'I cook dinner, I do housework, and besides, I have to take our daughter to all her appointments. While you're at work, I'm busy doing all this.' She felt justified in her behavior and actions because she truly did love her husband, but he was not satisfied. I got into his feelings about having an autistic child."

"What were those feelings?" I asked.

"He didn't really understand it. He thought it was very 'weird' that this had happened to him. He felt peculiar and disturbed about it because it contradicted his religious beliefs in terms of the way he felt about his child. He felt he should be more loving and more accepting of his child's disability. So we worked on that for a while to try to make him more accepting of his own feelings. The great thing about therapy is that you can talk about this stuff out in the open, and that seemed to be a big relief to him. But when they were together with me, the wife said to him, 'I just can't understand why you feel this way. That's the way our daughter is and she is going to be disabled the rest of her life and there is no cure for it.' And he finally said, 'I guess I could accept it if you'd get rid of that picture.' She said, 'Get rid of that picture, are you kidding?' Of course, I asked what picture they were talking about and they told me they had a hand-painted portrait of this child when she was three years old hanging on the wall over their bed. The wife thought it was a beautiful picture and I had to explain that it could make her husband feel a little uncomfortable if that was the picture she chose to hang over the bed. She said, 'Yes, but it's his child,' and I said, 'That's true, but he doesn't want to have her over the bed.'"

I told Dr. Eagle of my discussion with Lisa, the mother in the introduction to this section, who got so depressed over her life that she spent days unable to function. "All the issues with LD came to a head and she had a breakdown," I said. "My question is this: does depression come into it when you have a child with a disability?"

"Sure it does," said Dr. Eagle. "I think it's such a shock to a parent. The importance placed on learning and learning correctly has seeped down so that ordinary people who have a toddler who can't recognize an "A" start to get worried the child has a learning issue and then get depressed when the child can't get into the nursery school they hoped to get her into. And let's say in first grade the child is found to have LD. The parent who may have picked up on it early is a bit more prepared. But for the parent who did not pick up on it, it comes as a real shock — especially if they didn't have learning problems themselves. It's like being told your child has an illness you never expected."

"I know one or two fathers who are more involved with the disabled child than the wife, but that is not the usual situation. Do you find that it's mostly mothers?"

"Oh, yes, definitely," said Dr. Eagle. "That's the reality of what it is like out there, whether we like it or not. Women generally see themselves as responsible for their children. Are they eating well enough? Have they seen the doctor? Are they doing well in school? And men — even today they feel their job is to go out and earn money to support the family. That is still so prevalent."

"I remember one mother telling me that in their bedroom, the father has the remote control on his side of the bed and the mother has the stack of books on learning disabilities on hers."

"Absolutely," said Dr. Eagle. "I don't know what more I can say about this other than our culture still supports this. A man is really doing his job only if he is out there earning the money".

"Do you think that's true in every family?" I asked.

"No, not at all. But it's a cultural stereotype and I think that is what happens between men and woman. I also feel that if there is an obvious problem between couples over having a child with LD then there has to be something else going on between the couple. The disability becomes a point of focus where they can let it all out."

"So you think there is already another issue?"

"Yes. Nearly always there is something else going on. As an example, I knew a couple who fought about having a child. The husband didn't want to have the child right away due to financial reasons but the woman prevailed and they had a child. That child ended up having disabilities and so the financial burdens increased, and as a result they had real difficulties in the marriage."

"We have also heard about problems involving in-laws," I said, "especially when they don't believe there is anything going on with the child."

"Once again, therapy can help. Obviously I don't think there is any shame in talking to a therapist. It's such a resource that anybody can have at their fingertips. The mother who has the problem with the in-laws, or the father who has trouble with co-workers, is a person who needs support. They don't feel they can handle the problem on their own, and often they are right. They should be looking for support from literature, from books, from talking to other parents of children with LD, to make themselves feel better. It all has to do with the underlying feeling of 'how did I give birth to this disabled child? What happened? No one in my family has it. No one in the father's family has it. So how did this happen?' And no one knows the answer to that and there isn't going to be an answer for a long time. So the individual parent has to find support apart from the in-laws or unsupportive partner."

"I think the questions about why it happened never really go away. "

Dr. Eagle agreed: "Yes, they wonder if they did something wrong."

"Another thing we've found is that parents of children with LD often think they're the only ones going through it."

"Absolutely! Because they don't talk to others who are experiencing the same thing."

"We get this all the time. People write letters to us and say they don't feel so alone after reading our books. They are relieved to find they are not the only ones going through this."

"Sometimes they feel such shame about having a disabled child, and it's just terrible."

"I agree," I said. "And though it sounds terrible to say, sometimes it's easier to have a child with physical disabilities."

"Yes, because then you can't hide it and the world knows what is going on."

"We've talked to some mothers who have said they feel guilty because sometimes they've wished their children were more disabled. It would be easier for them to get the services they need, and society would probably be more understanding. Of course, they don't really mean they wish their child had more profound or pronounced disabilities, but you can understand their frustration."

"Yes, and we can use something like leukemia as an example. Generally you wouldn't immediately know a child has leukemia, but if I said to you, 'my child has leukemia and we don't know about the future,' you would feel very sorry for me and offer support. But if you say, 'my child has LD and we don't know about the future,' they'll say, 'oh, that's too bad,' and that's the end of it."

"So there are reasons they withdraw and don't talk about it," I said. "And it's a shame because there is support."

"There is tremendous support out there if you will accept it."

"So it could be your own sense of inadequacy that prevents you from seeking support."

"Yes. And let's not forget about rage. That's a big part of this too. Feeling angry over 'why did this happen to me? I didn't do anything wrong.'"

"Both parents feel this?" I asked.

"Yes. I think it's the psychology of it — to the degree that this child represents me is also the degree to which I'm ashamed, I'm embarrassed, I'm enraged, and I feel inadequate. The parent simply doesn't understand it."

"And they take the rage out on each other? Or on the child?"

"Sometimes on each other, sometimes on the child, yes."

"Wouldn't it also be important to identify the source of that rage? You're angry at the world, but you're not really aware that the reason you are angry is that you feel cheated because you didn't have the child you thought you'd have."

"And the child you dreamed of having," said Dr. Eagle. "I think most parents dream of the child they're going to have and it's terribly unsettling when they discover it's not going to be like that."

"They experience grief and disappointment."

"Exactly. And when groups of parents of children with disabilities get together they talk about mourning. It is part of the whole process of what one has to go through."

"The hardest part for me was dealing with the rejection by other children," I said. "My daughter had no friends. That didn't bother her so much, but it killed me. One parent told me not too long ago that they gave their child the choice about whether or not to play with Allegra. The child chose not to, and that was that. Allegra never saw that child again."

"It's a shame. They should have encouraged their child to play with Allegra."

"I couldn't agree more. Do you have any last things you would like to say?"

"I want to stress again that the most important thing is that the parent who is going through these difficulties needs support, and that the support is out there. They have to look for it because it is there. So many feel they are trapped and can't talk to anyone about their problems, and the mother or father will often weave shame and anger into the feeling of not being able to discuss it with anyone. This just makes the problem worse. If they could find a group of other parents who could talk about this, it would be helpful. They could go to group therapy or join a parent group such as LDA (Learning Disabilities Association of America.). Organizations such as that are not only for professionals in the field but also for the parents. There is help, and it is not difficult to find – you only have to take that first step and begin to look for it."

HOMEWORK: THE COMBAT ZONE

*H*omework.

For some of you, that word will bring up fond memories of sitting at the kitchen table with a parent, trying to figure out a math problem or working on a social studies essay. For others — mostly parents — the word will cause an involuntary shudder, especially as they remember the nightly battles with their children and the squabbles with their husband or wife, all due to this one not-so-simple evening routine.

I have seen reports by some professionals questioning the value of homework. I join them and the thousands (if not hundreds of thousands) of parents who do the same. Is this really worth all the heartache and aggravation? Does it really do any good? Does it truly help improve our children's grades and understanding? Wouldn't life be a whole lot easier and more peaceful if we could keep schoolwork in school where it belongs? In an interview with Clinical Psychologist Dr. Robert Brooks, he told me that he also questions the effectiveness of homework. He said, "One boy with LD told me, 'Going to school is like climbing Mount Everest every day without the right equipment and training, and then they ask you do to it again at night and they call it homework.'"

"Homework is always a difficult issue," I said.

"Yes, and parents should work closely with teachers to be very realistic about the amount of time spent on homework," Dr. Brooks told me. "I do have some questions about whether homework is really effective, especially in the elementary school years. There is some research that shows it does not enhance learning. And we also have to consider the kind of homework that is assigned. If it primarily involves rote learning, that format proves very difficult for kids with learning and attention problems. But assuming homework is here to stay, there should be a time limit on it and a consideration of what the homework involves. Also, homework should not be at the expense of the child's involvement with activities outside of the school. I also believe that parents should not be put in the position of having to monitor every little part of their child's day. I'm not saying there is an easy solution to the issue of homework. At an LDA conference in Texas, I heard a neurologist say that one of the biggest contributors to child abuse is homework. Of course he was joking, but the parents in the audience could relate and they laughed. The main point he was conveying was that homework leads to a lot of tension between children and their families, and it's not a very healthy situation."

Parents of high-achievers and academic stars may recoil at the thought of eliminating homework. In Allegra's early years at Gateway she had no homework at all. In her later years, she did — and speaking for myself, that homework was a chore, an ordeal, something so difficult I ended up referring to that end of the table where the homework was attempted as "the combat zone." We all know that children with LD have a difficult time in school, and it surely will not come as a surprise to discover the same challenges and frustrations when they bring out the book bag and homework assignments. They rebel, they delay, they procrastinate. Parents sometimes do the same, hoping if no one mentions it, the homework will somehow magically go away or, even better, do itself. Even when the child with LD truly wants to do homework, it may take two or three times longer to finish than it does for your other children.

When I spoke to parents about marital tensions and problems caused by a child's LD, I should have expected homework to come to the forefront of our discussions and I was not disappointed. Janie and Mark are the parents of three children, all three of whom have been diagnosed with LD or ADD and have

IEPs. Their eldest son Marky is thirteen. The younger son Luke is eleven and their daughter Grace is seven.

"It's difficult to talk about some of these family issues at a school meeting," Janie told me. "You don't want to bring the dynamics of your home life into the school. If you do, you sometimes feel you're being shamed because you can't get the situation under control."

"When you talk about the dynamics of your home, are you referring to sibling issues or problems between husbands and wives?" I asked.

"Both. In my case, the sibling problems and arguments with my husband almost always revolve around homework. Even though all of my children have been diagnosed with LD and all have IEPs, there are still problems amongst the siblings, especially if we go back a couple of years when my eldest Marky was the only one with a firm diagnosis. I had always assumed that my son Luke could handle his homework on his own. Because of that, I spent much more time with Marky — and it really was a lot of time. It was so much work just to get him to do the homework. Luke would say, 'You're always doing his homework. That's all you do. You care about him more.' So in Luke's world, he thought I was doing Marky's homework for him. He thought I cared more about Marky's grades. His thought process went like this: 'Marky can't do the homework so Mum does his homework every night and she doesn't care about me.' That has been a big problem, even after Luke himself was diagnosed with a learning disability. This battle went on every night, and I do mean every single night. Marky would say to me, 'I can't do it, I need you, I have to have your help,' and then Luke would say, 'Yup, why don't you just go do his homework again Mum.' And then my daughter Grace was also diagnosed with LD this year. I didn't really push her homework this year because I was trying to focus on Marky and Luke. It's a nightmare. That's what I would say about homework. When there is a learning disability in the home, homework is an absolute nightmare."

"Have you been able to find ways to lessen the nightmare?" I asked.

"Marky has been eligible for help at the library after school," Janie said. "It's called Homework Club, though it was a struggle to get him to attend. About halfway through seventh grade, I made a deal with the devil. I bribed him. I said, 'If you go, I'll buy you something.' So he went and he realized, 'Hey wait a minute...I can do my homework here where it's quiet. There are people here who are going to help me. This is great!' So homework became much better with Marky. Even so, there were those nights when, for whatever reason, he felt I needed to be at his side because that's what I've been doing all these years. We still have that situation from time to time. On top of this, Luke was diagnosed with ADD without the Hyperactivity. As of two days ago I started medicating him and I fought with my husband for five years about it."

"So let's move on to that," I said. "In your case, sibling issues and marital issues seem to blend together. I do not mean to bash husbands, but in many cases the mother takes the brunt of the difficulties."

"I agree," Janie said. "It's the role we play. We set ourselves up for it. In many cases, they go to work, they make the money…that's not to say many women don't work. Of course, many, if not most, women do work."

"Which brings about its own set of difficulties and concerns," I said.

"Always," Janie agreed. "But I don't have a full time job, so I felt at the end of the day it was my role to make sure everything is done when my husband comes through that door."

"And have you had any difficulties with that?"

"Oh yes! The difficulties have been going on for years. Basically, this is the problem. My husband Mark will call on his way home from work and say, 'How's the homework? Is it done?' and instantly, I'm angry. It's like he turns a switch on. I want to hang up on him. At this stage of the game, it's not first grade homework anymore. We're dealing with middle school homework and we have three kids with LD, so when my husband calls and says that, I immediately get nasty and say things like, 'They're your children too and we need more than one person to sit here and help with the homework.'"

"How does he respond?" I asked.

"He'll say they're capable of doing their homework on their own, even though they have all been diagnosed with something and are simply *not* capable of doing it on their own. He is still in denial there is a learning disability involved."

"Still?"

"Can you believe that?" Janie asked. "He has three children with disabilities, but he is still in denial. He knows it on one level, but on another level he still thinks they can fight it or it can be cured. Is that not crazy?"

"It's more common than you think," I said. "And though there are always exceptions, we tend to find more denial among men than women. That's not to say some woman can't experience denial. I only have to look in the mirror to find one who did, and it never works out in the end. Never. I can't think of a single case where denying a disability of any kind did anything except cause additional problems."

"Exactly," Janie said. "And with some men, it's as if they are saying, "that can't be happening, not with *my* children." But my husband Mark tends to see them in a different light. I see their weaknesses. He sees their strengths."

"Do you feel that is a good thing?"

"It is, but he sometimes takes it too far. He wants them to overcome this and be rid of it. I keep saying they're going to find tools to help them compensate, but this is with them for life. That's where we battle. He doesn't quite believe it."

"I'm getting the sense that he dreads the whole homework issue too."

"He does!" Janie said. "He absolutely dreads it. It is a thorn in his side. He'll come home and I'll say, 'If you could sit with Luke, and I could sit with Marky...' and of course he will, don't get me wrong. He really will. But he's always like, 'Really? It's not done? They've had since three o'clock and it's now five o'clock.'"

"Some people would never believe homework can be such a battleground."

"It really is. If someone asked me to choose one thing in my life that I consider a problem, I would really have to say it's that — homework. I'm already dreading September. I really am. I always dread the start of the school year. I dread the fact that it is all going to start again."

"Is your husband dreading it too?"

"Without question," Janie said. " It's a nightmare for both of us. Marky is going into eighth grade. This has been going on since first grade. Sometimes I come back at him and say, 'You just want to come home only after I say the coast is clear.'"

"Does your husband always ask about the homework?"

"Always. If he didn't ask me on the phone, he will come home and before even saying hello, he'll sometimes say, 'Is your homework done?' At the same time, he knows what it takes to get it done and he doesn't want to engage in it. But he does enjoy our children — he is the greatest dad. He takes them hiking, if there is a game he's there — he always has fun with the kids."

"It is important for our readers to know that this is a normal guy," I said. "He loves his children. He's a good father. This is not a bad guy."

"Oh no, not at all!" Janie said. "He works six days a week. He provides for us so I don't have to work. He never says no to them. We have our limits of course, but he's a great father. And I'm not saying this because he's my husband – he truly is an amazing father."

"And even wanting them to do homework shows he's interested," I said. "It could be very easy for some husbands to give up and say, 'I don't care.'"

"And I don't blame them," Janie said with a laugh. "Sometimes I feel that way!"

"You feel like giving up?"

"Of course. I ask them to do their homework, they complain, and I'll say something like, 'OK, whatever, just don't do it then.' Or, rather, I *want* to say it but I usually don't."

"There are a lot of people who feel that way, I'm sure."

"Yes, because it's an easy out. And I can bash myself a little bit here…I say my husband doesn't want to engage in the whole ordeal, but I have to admit that sometimes the homework doesn't get done because I don't feel like engaging in the battle either. I don't want to have to sit there and focus and help three kids do homework. Maybe the problem is me! Maybe it's me because I'm thinking, 'Oh my God, I have to sit here *again* and fight with three kids to get their homework done.' I think to myself, 'I don't feel like doing this right now. It's too much. I don't want to sit down and do it.' So it's not always my husband. We each have a role."

"And I think that is a very human thing," I said. "This is a daily battle and I think you both probably want vacations from it."

"No question about it," Janie said. "And sometimes I don't want to push it because it isn't pleasant. I want them to be kids. I want them to have fun. But then time slips away and it's not done and then suddenly the kids are blaming me and saying, 'You should have told me earlier, I would have done it, but now it's eight o'clock and I can't do it, I'm too tired.'"

"The kids blame you because they didn't do their homework?"

"Of course! They'll say I should have told them to do it, or blame me if I wasn't home to help them. That's the biggest thing I get. And as we're talking, I realize that it's true – I *do* want to escape from it all too."

"I don't blame you," I said with a laugh.

"I really do have to help them with everything, so at the end of the day I'm burnt out. I don't want to redo English and math. I did my time, you know?

So it takes up a couple of hours of my day, every day, to do it. Sometimes I just want to escape!"

I told Janie that it sounded like she had a really great relationship with her children and her husband in spite of the constant homework struggle.

"Oh yes, I do," she said. "At the end of the day, we're all on the same page," she said. "We want to be happy and we want everyone to be happy. We had our denial issues for a while, thinking LD couldn't happen in our family. But then we had all the reports — no one just labels your kids as having LD for the fun of it. So my husband is pretty good about it all now. We all are. We all do our part, trying the best we can to live in harmony."

The challenges of homework came up in my conversation with another couple, Laura and Kimo, who have a son named Ethan who has LD. I asked them if they had ever had any difficulties when it came time to do homework.

"Oh yes," Laura said without hesitation. "Think about it: every parent wants their child to do well in school. This is where they're spending eight hours of their day. I've had to accept that I can't let my children's grades be a reflection of who I am, but that's a human notion. When you have kids you want them to be perfect little reflections of everything you do well, and you want them to exhibit it to the world. You have to deal with that when you have kids. When they're bringing home paperwork that looks terrible and low grades, and you know what it's being held up against — it's hard. In Ethan's formative years, we gave him a lot of early intervention and support in early reading. We anticipated that reading was going to be the major problem, but when he got to third grade, he hit the wall in math."

"How so? Memorizing times tables?"

"Yes, that became a huge problem. There were timed quizzes, memorization; all the things that happened in math at that particular time caused real problems. We had him evaluated. He didn't meet the requirements to get an IEP, so he has what's called a 504 Plan. He doesn't meet our county's High IQ/ Low Achievement discrepancy requirement, which means he has a high IQ but he doesn't have low enough achievement. But we were never going to let him go there. You have to fall two grade levels behind to qualify! Of course, we weren't going to ever let him fail to that degree so we got him a 504 Plan and then we got him a tutor. The tutor was meant to give instructional support in these areas that were becoming a major issue, but what happened was this: he wanted to start taking his homework to work on with the tutor. She was great. We had her for three years, and it created this nice buffer so that when we were helping him with his homework, he already knew in his mind the things he was going to do with Mom and Dad and what he was going to do with Sherry, the tutor. It took a layer of tension off us to have that dynamic. My husband and I have different approaches to homework. I'll let Kimo speak for himself, but I have to remember that my son Ethan's brain doesn't work like mine. He doesn't automatically get it. He's not going to remember this tomorrow. That is an ongoing dilemma for me. And for him to not have us always looking over his shoulder and do it with him was a really nice thing. When he did homework with the tutor, there was no judgment — he didn't have that parent pressure he resented going on. That helped us minimize the ugliness of homework and it fostered independent thinking and planning by Ethan that we never anticipated — an unplanned benefit. It was worth every dollar we sacrificed elsewhere in the budget to pay for it."

Laura's husband Kimo also has learning disabilities and had his own challenges with homework while growing up. "And how do you deal with your son's homework issues?" I asked.

"Having the tutor was huge because it changed the dynamic. I had a specific way that I learned to do homework and, with him, I was using that same model. It was the Drill and Kill method, doing the same thing over and over. I had to get away from that because that wasn't what Ethan needed and it created all kinds of negative interactions between us. The tutor also helped me understand that he needs to see broad concepts, and by teaching him those broad concepts first, then you can drill down to the smaller ideas. She also gave us different ways to teach, for example, multiplication tables. He's not going to remember 3×3 is 9, 4×4 is 16. He is just not going to remember that unless he can see it. So we took out pennies and used them, where three sets of three are nine."

"Did it help?"

"Yes," Kimo said. "We had a money box and we played with money to help, and we also used buttons. We had to figure out how to visually and tactilely put forward and reinforce these concepts so they would go into long term memory. This big picture and tactile approach has been essential to his learning in more than just math."

We should not think of the homework battle as one that is destined to be lost. Couples need to come up with creative approaches. In my conversation with

Dr. Carol Eagle, she said, *"Any* homework can cause strife and conflict between parents - not only homework for children with LD. It may seem like a minor issue, but for some couples, it is the big problem in their lives."

I asked if she had any advice for these parents.

"First, I think that people get into trouble when they think that homework with a child with LD is automatically more difficult than doing homework with a child without LD," said Dr. Eagle. "I try to get them to understand that it's not more difficult, but it is different from *our* way of learning. The challenge for the parent or the therapist is to find out how the child learns. They learn differently than the mother or father. One approach, for example, is for the mother to say, 'We're stumbling over this page and I don't understand why I can't reach you and you can't reach me about it. Explain it to me.' The mother would attempt to see where the child is coming from. So you take their position intellectually and try to understand where they're coming from — but this does not mean you accept their position. Many people get so discouraged with the homework. It can confound the whole dynamic of the family when so much is focused on homework. I also think it is very important for all of us to try to stretch our own minds in an attempt to understand where the child is coming from and how the child learns."

"That would apply to all children, whether they have a disability or not," I said. "Homework would be so much easier if you know how the child is trying to approach the issue rather than using the cookie-cutter approach to force all children into doing things the same way."

"Exactly," said Dr. Eagle. "And if a chocolate chip cookie persuades you to spend a half an hour more on homework, then you should get a chocolate chip cookie. I see this as perfectly legitimate."

"And what about the couple who only have one specific problem, like homework, but everything else in their family life is fine? They have minor issues, but they are mostly a happy, loving, well-adjusted couple. How do they deal with that one difficult issue?"

"Let me talk from a therapist's point of view," said Dr. Eagle. "If I saw these two in therapy, I would ask them, 'What is so terrible about the homework and why do one of you have such a difficult time with it. I would really try to get into it to try to understand exactly what it is. Let's say the father is the one with the problem. Is it due to his wife's attitude towards the child? Is it the child's attitude toward the mother, that the father can't stand that interaction? Or is it something that affects him, such as the necessity that everyone be quiet in the house so the child can do the homework? I would look very hard at trying to understand the difficulties caused by this child doing homework. I would hate to hear (and unfortunately it is something I would expect to hear in some cases) that the mother yells at the child and it makes the father very anxious because his own mother used to yell at him like that. A good suggestion might be to have the wife try to look at the experience from her husband's point of view so she can try to understand what is going on. If he says, 'It's the way you're talking to him when I come home, it's driving me crazy,' she will probably understand."

"Obviously the roles can be reversed in all these examples," I said. "We could easily be talking about the mother who comes home after a hard day's work and faces the same issues. But let's stick to the husband coming home from work and says, 'I work all day. I want to come home and relax. I'm not going to do the homework.'"

"Well, there again, only in therapy can you work through this, but I would suggest that homework not be done at that time. Homework could be done either earlier before Dad gets home, or Dad comes home and they have a lovely family dinnertime together, and then the homework is done. Of course a lot of this then falls on the mother. I think the burdens of some of this can lead to depression, fatigue, and a lot of resentment against the husband who won't support her. The mother says, 'who told me I was going to have to be a teacher again?' People who have these resentments and feelings need to be worked with. They need to be told, 'Get it out. Talk to somebody about it.' This is going to color everything, and it snowballs."

"It does," I said, "and it's going to happen for eighteen years."

"Exactly!"

Nearly every family struggles at some point with the homework dilemma. Children go through developmental and educational shifts and, as experts have pointed out, there are keys to navigating it, especially for families with children diagnosed with learning disabilities.

Here are a few things to consider:

TIME

Set aside a specific time each day that everyone knows is homework time. Take short breaks during homework time if you need to, and negotiate together to make a plan that you can adapt and adjust as needed. Allow downtime *before and after* homework time so that both the child and parents have time to play, relax, unwind, regroup and mentally be ready to focus on the task.

TUTORS

If possible, hiring other people to teach and support your child can be well worth it. Parents must first be sure of the purpose of hiring a tutor. If it is to truly supplement the teaching process outside of school, the tutor must be familiar with the grade level curriculum and grade level standards/expectations in your school and district. The tutor must have knowledge of the child's disability and how it affects learning and behavior. They should be professional in their approach and able to create a teacher–student bond with your child that both you and your child trust and respect. Asking for references at the school from the special education staff, or from friends who also have children with LD can lead to a good and affordable match. You must be in frequent contact to assure the tutor is truly helping your child progress academically while, at the same time, communicate with your child about how it is going on a regular basis.

RESPECT

Parents need to come to an understanding about their child's strengths and weaknesses, and approach homework time with these in mind. This sets everyone up emotionally to have a more positive interaction. Trying to look at things from the child's point of view is essential. It is also important to know how a brain with a processing disorder takes in the information and what it needs to do to retain and retell it. Badgering and nagging your child doesn't typically help and parents will need to gauge whether a child will respond to a reward or reward system that may be designed and negotiated together. Parents frustrated with the family schedule and the stress placed on everyone by homework must take that frustration to a private place and/or therapy. Most importantly, the child needs to see a united front and a team approach when possible. Do not minimize the stress caused by homework! You do not need to suffer, nor does your child. Talk to someone. Find help. There are answers to your specific situation.

LAURA AND KIMO

Coping with LD as a Couple

*I*n my years as Chairman of the National Center for Learning Disabilities, I worked with Laura Kaloi (who we heard from in the Homework chapter, along with her husband Kimo). Laura was NCLD's Director of Public Policy for many years, and in that role, Laura led initiatives to establish NCLD as a lead voice and critical partner in education policy impacting all major federal education legislation from 1999-2013. She also led the development of online and social media advocacy tools and trained thousands of parents to be a voice for their own child. She is now a Vice President at Washington Partners, a government affairs firm where she helps clients achieve education policy and public relations success.

Laura's husband, Kimo Kaloi, Esq., is Director, U.S. Department of the Interior, Office of Native Hawaiian Relations, where he helps federal officials more effectively carry out their responsibilities for Native Hawaiian affairs in Hawaii and the Pacific region.

We have already heard from them in the chapter about Homework, but I asked that they join me for a broader discussion. They are the proud parents of three children who attend the Virginia public schools: Mahea age 17, Ethan age 14, and Hannah age 11. Their son Ethan was diagnosed with learning disabilities and, as a couple, they have worked through the various options for ensuring his success. What makes their story unique and instructive for other couples is that Kimo Kaloi also has a diagnosed learning disability and the presence of LD in both father and son has made for some interesting insights.

Laura and Kimo traveled to New York from Washington DC to talk with me and I began our discussion by asking them about LD as it relates to their family. "Kimo, you have learning disabilities," I said.

"Yes, I was diagnosed when I was in fourth grade and again when I was in college. I have dyslexia and dysgraphia, which means I have difficulty with both reading and writing. Sometimes it's difficult to put on paper what I have in my thoughts."

"And did you get accommodations?"

"Not in grade school. I grew up and went to school in Hawaii. I wasn't getting accommodations and I was failing everything. The school was essentially saying, 'oh, he's just a stupid Hawaiian kid, no big deal.' I remember being asked what I wanted to be when I grew up. I said I wanted to be an attorney and the teacher told me, 'I think you're setting your sights a little too high. Maybe you could be a janitor.' I was only nine years old but I got really mad and I thought, 'I'll show you — I'm going to become an attorney.' I think dealing with these sorts of low expectations is one of the things you face when you also have LD: in order to overcome it, you have to be stubborn and you have to be willing to not let anyone put you in a box. That's what drove me my whole life, not letting anyone else define me. When I was in fifth grade, my grandfather dropped me off at school. That was a turning point because he was the former executive secretary of the Teachers Union and one of the teachers saw him and knew who he was. That's when I started getting accommodations and testing. I can remember getting these tests and being told, 'You have dyslexia which means you can't read well, and you have a difficult time with short term memory. But you are operating at a tenth grade level for vocabulary and math. And we don't really completely understand what's going on.' There was something wrong with the way I was processing things, and discovering that was liberating. I was finally able to put a label on it and say, 'OK, I have an issue. I just need to figure out a way to cope with it.' I gave myself a little more time and I stopped beating myself up over the fact that I couldn't read as fast as everybody else. There was also an issue with the way the teachers treated me – I wasn't doing well in class. I was failing everything, and the way the teacher decided she was going to motivate me was to tell me I couldn't go out for recess. She locked me in the room. This happened a number of times. I had to stay inside while everybody else went out for recess." Kimo paused for a moment, still affected by the memory after all these years. "I never even thought to tell my parents about that," he finally said.

"I was going to ask you what your parents thought about all this."

"They didn't really know," Kimo said. "They were going through a divorce at the time. We didn't have a whole lot of money. My mother was on food stamps for quite a while. But the treatment by the teacher was one of those actions that fueled me later. I would say to myself, 'I don't care what you do to me. I'm going to figure this out.'

Laura said, "Also when Kimo was in eighth grade, the school had a meeting with his mother and told her not to expect him to graduate from high school and that they should start making plans for him. I didn't know any of this before we got married."

"Did you know he had dyslexia?" I asked.

"I knew he had dyslexia, but I didn't know anything about dyslexia. I just thought it had to do with reading and school. I didn't know it would affect the fabric of our life and our relationship."

"How did it do that?"

"It took some time for that to happen," Laura said. "Kimo was in law school very early in our relationship, and there was a lot of lonely time in those two years. I was supportive, but he made it clear when he got into law school that he had to study eight to ten hours a day in addition to going to class. So imagine the hours we spent apart, especially in his first year of law school. He said to me that he felt like a little guy with a bucket and shovel standing in front of a big mountain that he had to cut through. That image helped me see that he was trying to make a plan to either climb over the mountain or dig through it with his little bucket and shovel."

"This was before any children?" I asked.

"Yes," Laura said. "We didn't have our daughter until we'd been married for three years. It was his last year of law school. I was finishing my masters and went to school at night. He went to school during the day and studied at night."

"I was really worried about being able to pass my classes," Kimo said. "It was a difficult thing."

Laura said, "So then I came to NCLD and I started reading about all this, and I started thinking...hmmm. One day I happened to talk to one of my co-workers about someone who had called about the challenges of math and the processing issues involved with how money works. My co-worker asked if this was a struggle for my husband and suddenly this huge light bulb went off in my head and I thought, 'Is *that* why he can't manage our checkbook?' All of a sudden it all came to light."

"He has troubles with math?" I asked.

"He doesn't have math problems," Laura said, "but what he has is a processing delay. For instance, in our early years, we were on a tight budget. There was a time when we had to decide how much to pay on one bill versus another bill. It was juggling the priorities and it was that kind of decision making that was a challenge. It wasn't whether to pay the bills or who to pay them to or how to write the checks; but it was the executive function connected to all of the moving parts and the decision-making that had to occur. So that was one of my first insights when I realized this is more than just reading."

"And you never saw this before you got married?"

"No. We dated for nine months and we were engaged for nine months, and we were in love! When you're falling in love, you don't see any of those things."

"Plus I was really good-looking," Kimo added.

"Oh, you still are, Kimo," I said.

"He also struggles to make eye contact," Laura said. "He's very good at knowing he needs to make eye contact — and he will. But, as he explained to me, he has to look away because his brain is trying to catch up. I can move a million miles a minute. That's who I am and how I function. I have to remember he is not that. It's taught me that I have to slow down. I'll admit that sometimes I'll say to him, 'You gotta speed up.' An ongoing part of our conversations is about how to communicate without creating misunderstandings that are unnecessary."

"And when you communicate, do you both agree?" I asked. "For instance, Kimo, if Laura brings up the issue with eye contact, will you listen?"

"Oh yes," he said. "I completely agree."

"That can be difficult to take sometimes, hearing such things."

"We had that conversation a long time ago," Laura said. "So we're both used to it now."

"What is really great about this, and what will be a great lesson for anyone reading it, is how open you both are about all this."

"Things unfolded over time," Laura said.

"And what is the process? How did you get there?"

Kimo said, "From my side, I've always been looking for ways to break out of that box and to compensate. I do my best. It's hard to take criticism from your spouse, from someone you love and care about and respect. So it didn't happen all at once. It unfolded. Little things here and there were discussed. Even at work, in the interview process…it was difficult for me, partly because of this whole eye contact thing."

"Having a spouse who is aware of their own issues and accepting of them is rather important," I said. "It makes things so much easier. If you're in self-denial, the other one can't say anything to you about the problems and challenges of LD, and nothing can get done about it."

Kimo said, "I think it's really important for parents of kids with LD to talk to their kids about their disability so they will accept it. Ever since I was nine or ten years old, I've had to acknowledge it and say, 'I have a problem and here are some solutions,' and to continue to look for the solutions. That's what I've been doing most of my life. I try to be open to suggestions, especially if they're given in a constructive manner. If Laura had come to me in an accusatory way and said, 'You really need to start looking at people', I would probably have rebelled. But she did it in a way where it was a safe environment. It wasn't critical. It was trying to help. There were times when she would ask, 'Why aren't you looking at me?' and that's when I said, 'I can't process so much information at once. I can't process the visual and I can't process the auditory at the same time or it gets all jumbled up.'"

I asked Laura, "As a wife or husband who is trying to talk to his or her spouse about an issue, what is the best approach?"

"We've been to therapy a couple of times," Laura said. "I've gone myself over the years. One thing my therapist said one time — and, frankly, it was the most helpful thing anyone's ever said to me — was, 'Remember, with every sentence you say to him, you can understand every sound and syllable you say; but just imagine if all of the As and Bs were missing. That's what it's like for him. He's trying to put it all together. His brain works differently than your brain.' For me, that little metaphor did it. I really understood, though I still have to remind myself at times. We get caught up in life. We have three kids, we have two jobs, we have two dogs — we have a busy life! We have the same challenges as any married couple in trying to figure out how to spend time together and talk and stay connected in a way that helps our relationship grow. I have to remind myself to be patient. As I said, I'm a mover and I sometimes have to remember to slow down. And then we also have our son who also has LD."

"What was his diagnosis?" I asked.

"He has dyslexia and dysgraphia, the same as Kimo," Laura said.

"We often hear that LD runs in families — this is a great example."

"Yes, it is. The first signs we had were at age three when he needed speech therapy. He did not learn to speak and articulate his words in a normal pattern. That was our first indication that he might have inherited the processing issues from Kimo, and so we started on a path at age three with him. We've watched all three of our children closely because LD is not gender exclusive, but our other two do not have LD."

"How old is your son now?" I asked.

"He's thirteen."

WORKING THROUGH LD AS A COUPLE

"We've heard how you're working through Kimo's LD as a couple, but how are you working through your son's LD as a couple? You've obviously accepted it, but was there any conflict about treatment or what to do about it?"

"There have been discussions about what to do," Kimo said. "We bounce ideas off each other about it. One of my biggest issues that I always try to be aware of is that he is not me. He doesn't have the exact same issues I have, so the tricks I used for myself don't always work for him. Sometimes they do. I think one of the big bonuses for me and for all of us is that I'm not in denial about it."

"You understand it," I said.

"Yes. But before we understood what was going on, it was a little bit difficult. When he was very young we knew something wasn't quite right. We would keep going over and over something, drilling it over and over, hoping he would eventually get it, but he didn't. It wasn't until recently that he was able to memorize our phone number. Mind you, this is a kid who is in Honors classes, but he couldn't remember his own phone number and still can't remember his home address. We've taught him some tricks, mnemonics and such, and that has helped."

Laura added, "And keep in mind, the dynamics of Kimo's family life and our family's life. We've had a research-based instructional approach to helping Ethan that Kimo didn't have. Kimo really had to wing it. His parents didn't know what to do. The school system didn't know what to do. This was the 70s and 80s. The Special Ed law was so new. They knew he had something. He was clearly diagnosed, there was enough data, but they didn't know what to do about it. And even though the schools still don't quite know what to do, we have a different set of resources to work around that. Also, when Ethan was really little, we said things to him like 'you struggle with this and we're going to help you figure it out.' We said stuff like that. But when we actually got the diagnosis when he was nine, we sat down with him and told him about his disability. That was really sad for Kimo."

"It probably brought up things about your own childhood," I said to Kimo.

"I didn't want him to have to deal with the things I've had to deal with all my life," he said. "He has different tools at his disposal now, but it's not an easy road.

"We sat down with Ethan and the person who did the evaluation," Laura said. "She was terrific. She said, 'This is how your brain works. You get the big picture. You love big ideas, you can talk about them, although you're going to struggle with things that have to be done in order.' Ethan asked, 'Is that why I can't remember my address or my phone number?' And we said, yes, that's why you struggle with that."

"It's interesting," I said. "She gave the accomplishments first."

"Yes, and she was great about that."

"She first focused on the things he does really well."

"Did he have special accommodations?" I asked.

"For taking a test, yes. He had a private room for that. But he doesn't have an IEP so he didn't get any support in the school. That is the distinct difference between the IEP and the 504 plan. When you have a 504 Plan you only get accommodations, which means extra time, etc. But they don't give any extra instructional support. You can demand instructional services through the IEP."

"And how is he doing now?"

"He is now thirteen, and we just had his parent/teacher meeting last week with the school. I came home and talked to Ethan about it and asked how he was doing with his LD. He said, 'Mom, I've embraced the dyslexia because it forced me to learn how to read and I love to read.' And he does! We can tell you stories about twenty charges to Amazon in a row to download book after book."

"That's where a $160 Amazon charge came from this past summer," Kimo said.

"And how do you punish a kid with dyslexia for downloading twenty books on his Kindle?" Laura asked. "He followed up his line about dyslexia with, 'But I hate the dysgraphia.' So the full quote was, 'I've embraced the dyslexia because I love to read, but I hate the dysgraphia.' Dysgraphia is not only writing issues — it's also a processing issue."

"Does the computer help?" I asked.

"Yes, the computer helps tremendously because you don't have to deal with the actual mechanics of writing, which are the true issue with dysgraphia. But because he has the processing challenge, he's having to take the long way around to actually write down the thoughts he has. So how it translates is this: he has a tremendous vocabulary. He's a funny, terrific kid. He can tell great stories. When he was in fifth grade, he said he wanted to have a book on the New York Times bestseller list. That's one of his goals. But when he writes, the great vocabulary words are left out. They are in his head when he wants to say them, but when he writes the sentence, it gets truncated down. The sentence 'It's a beautiful, bright, sunny day in New York City' turns into 'The sun was out.'"

Kimo said, "The perception of him socially is that he performs at a high level. He's good looking, he speaks well, and has high social skills, so sometimes the teachers forget that he has LD. This means that sometimes things don't match up for them. If we hadn't been saying anything to them, he probably would have just been passed on. He could easily fall through the cracks."

Laura said: "He could probably get by without the help we've been giving him, but he isn't just getting by. He's an A and B student."

"So you're saying the teachers can't believe there's anything wrong," I said.

"They struggle with it," Laura said.

"What is the relationship between Ethan and his sisters?" I asked.

Kimo said, "He doesn't feel he needs to compete with his older sister. They're four years apart. There's a nice close relationship between the two and they're becoming better friends. With his younger sister, Hannah — she's smart and very athletic and high-functioning socially, and he feels he has to compete with her. She comes very close to being at his same grade level in a lot of different things. It's only recently when he's surpassed her in sports and in some of the other schoolwork, but she pushes herself to try to keep up with him and that makes it hard."

"The other two children don't complain about the attention?"

"They never have," Laura said. "We were talking about this on the train up here. When Ethan was younger, he got a lot of attention. Let's put it this way - no one's ever been vocal about it."

"Do you ever bring it up to them?"

"Yes. And we talk about Kimo's LD too."

I said, "When we talk to adults who had a sibling with LD, they say that talking about it would have helped enormously — just acknowledging that something is going on."

"It's interesting how many people we know, through church, through sports, through school and through work who have some dynamic related to a disability in their lives," Laura said. "Sometimes I ask those I know fairly well if they are talking about it with their family — the different responses are really interesting. If you're not talking about it as a couple, that's one challenge. If you're not talking with the child, that's another challenge. And then the whole family is another challenge. We've embraced the idea that we all have to be talking about it. Sometimes it isn't easy. Hannah, our youngest, is probably the most jealous of the attention. But she's also the type that if you gave her attention 24/7, it still wouldn't be enough. When Ethan had a tutor, she wanted one, even though she didn't need one."

"Many parents don't realize there is a problem between siblings when one has LD. They just assume it's obvious that the one child needs additional help."

Laura said, "I think our older daughter is so intuitive that she just knew he needed something that she didn't, and she's absorbed that it is fine."

COPING IN THE MARRIAGE

Laura said, "What I would say about how we cope in our marriage is we have to keep talking about the various challenges associated with LD. Having Ethan is a blessing in a way because it gives us a new way to talk about it. I'll give you another example. When I got married, I thought, 'I'll never be one of those wives who writes lists.' That's not me. Well, I had to learn that two people in my life need lists. They need them for organization at home and to keep our lives in some kind of order. They both need help with that. I've had to own that that is part of my job. It's my job because they are people who I love and I chose them to be in my life, and I just had to get over it."

"What was your problem with that?" I asked. "I live with lists!"

"I didn't want to be doing it for other people," Laura said. "I do it for myself. I didn't want to do it for Kimo — and I don't do it for everything. He functions quite well independent of me, but I had to recognize that they need lists in order to help them be more organized. It's a skill that I have, to be a planner, to be thinking ahead. It's part of what I bring to the dynamic that both of them need."

"Are you understanding of that?" I asked Kimo. "You don't mind the lists?"

"I welcome it," he said. "I admit, at work I have to force myself to be hyper-organized because if I'm not, then things don't get done. But I can't maintain that all day, 24/7. It usually ends up stopping at the door."

"What has been the greatest challenge in the family, the one that just keeps going on?" I asked.

"I think the organization issues are the ones that drive me the most crazy," Laura said. "I'll give you a good example. Our pantry. Canned goods are clearly in a distinct place in the pantry. Boxes of cereal are very clearly in a distinct place in the pantry. It's not super-organized, I'm not one of those people who label everything, but it's orderly. But honestly, if I let the two of them try to organize the pantry, it would be just shoving things here and there and not putting things back where they belong."

"The other two kids aren't like that?"

"No. And it's not a blame game. We're trying to deal with it. My son's room is an example. We're trying to get him into better habits. Kids struggle with this. Our other kids struggle with this too. But he in particular struggles with where to put stuff."

"When you tell him something does he retain it?" I asked.

"No. That's part of the problem. Because of my job, I do a lot of reading about and understanding the research behind dyslexia and the science of brain research. Some people in that world don't agree that these executive function issues such as organization and time management are real for people with dyslexia. But they are! I live with it. I see it. Neither my son nor husband have been diagnosed with or have attention issues. So it's the way the brain processes information. And living with it, I see that dyslexia does affect executive function."

"And we can define executive function as involving such things as planning, organizing, strategizing, paying attention to and remembering details, and managing time."

"That's right. And in our family, organization is the biggest challenge with executive function."

THE BENEFITS OF THERAPY

"Now getting back to therapy," I said. "If a couple is having trouble with the marriage or with children due to the LD, you suggest going to therapy. What type of therapist would you look for? The therapist who helped you obviously had some insight into the effects of LD on a family."

Laura said, "She was a licensed therapist but she was also someone who was qualified to do private evaluations. I learned of her through an LD network, so she did have experience working with, evaluating, and determining learning problems because she had an educational background. She became a therapist after she did some work in education."

"So it's not a specific type of therapy she practiced."

"No. She just happened to have a nice intersection of work experience with our needs. But my advice is that kids can take over your entire life."

"They can suck the marrow out of your bones," Kimo said with a laugh.

"And you have to figure out how to stay connected as a couple," Laura said. "No matter what your challenge is, you have to find someplace where you can go and discuss those challenges. If LD is a layer on top of that, look for someone who would have knowledge and at least an interest and an understanding. It shouldn't be someone who, for instance, thinks LD is just something you grow out of, or that it isn't real. If you have someone like that, they're not going to deal with the actual, neurological processing that's going on. So understanding the premise that it's real, it's lifelong, and that it changes and evolves is important."

"That's what I meant," I said. "In the case of marriage therapy for a couple where one has LD, it would seem pointless to go to someone who doesn't understand LD or take it seriously. Otherwise that therapist might only side with the husband or wife who doesn't have LD."

Laura said, "It's probably best to find someone who works with families and/or children who have special needs. They have to have a grounding in that."

"How would you find someone?" I asked. "Do you interview them?"

"Yes," Laura said. "Try a session with two or three people, and have your criteria when you go in. I have a couple of other criteria that deal with the framework of who I am as a person. It would be difficult to change certain things about how I'm coming at an issue or problem because of how I've been raised or things that I believe. So going into a discussion with a therapist, you would say, 'You need to know up front these three or four things about me, and are you comfortable with that? One of them is, we have learning disabilities in our family, and they're real, and they are part of the fabric of our life, and I want to be able to talk about them.' See what the reaction is to that."

CONSTRUCTIVE CRITICISM

"Any last things you would like to discuss?" I asked.

Kimo said, "One of the things Laura suggested that I mention is some of the volunteer work that I do. I work with a youth sports organization in Virginia. One of the things you see is the LD in kids coming out through sports, whether it be ADHD, dyslexia, or Aspergers."

"Do you coach kids because they have LD or are they kids who just happen to have it?" I asked.

"They just happen to have it. When I was new at basketball coaching, they put all the kids with any sort of behavioral issues on my team. So out of a team of eight kids, I had five who had issues. Three had ADHD, one had Aspergers with major social challenges, and one had behavior issues. It was difficult. We were trying to find resources and I would talk to the parents to try to find out what to do. And then you discover that some of the parents don't give the kids their medication for basketball practice. Or you find that that they're completely oblivious to it, or they have it themselves so they don't really pay attention. I also help administer the program. We have between 1400 and 2000 kids. What I've seen is that when you try to talk to the parents about the issue, you have to be very careful. You can't just come out and say you know the child has some issue or other, because I don't know for sure. I'm not a professional. Even so, you can tell when kids are having issues when they're on your team. The moms are usually the ones who are a lot more open to discussing it."

"Would this have been the first time some of the parents have talked about it?" I asked.

"It varies," Kimo said. "With some, their kids do well in school but can't pay attention at all on the team."

"Did you find the fathers were in denial or more resistant than the mothers?"

"Yes," Kimo said. "With some of them it was like hitting a brick wall. Especially when it came to the boys. With daughters, it was a little softer. But with boys, it was hitting a brick wall to talk to the fathers. I don't know how many times I've had to deal with this issue — I've lost count. But it's an interesting dynamic. It's also important with these kids to sandwich any criticism with compliments, and the compliments have to be real. You can't just say, 'You did a really good job — but.' You should never use the word 'but' in your criticism. And I realized, if I can do that with the kids in my volunteer work, I really needed to be doing it with my own kids too."

"What do you do instead of criticizing?" I asked.

"For instance, I'll say, 'Johnny, you're doing a great job with hand positioning when dribbling the ball. I really need you to be looking up so that you can see where the defenders are. What's great, though, is that you can keep the ball away from them because of the way you control it.' So you sandwich the critical point between two compliments."

Laura said, "He's had kids who have behavior disorders. Using strategies of balancing compliments and criticism, he's seen some real improvement. But the other thing is that he does this at home too."

"These are teaching strategies that should be used everywhere," Kimo said. "They help all kids. No one wants to be told they're really awful at something."

"It's the same with school meetings," Laura said. "It is difficult when you go in and all you hear about is what the child is doing wrong, and what you are doing wrong. There's so much pushback to make it the kid's fault instead of trying to figure out ways to support the child so he or she can be successful. But you know what? We're not perfect parents. No one is."

"Any last things you want to say?"

"I'd like to say one last thing about Kimo that I think is so great," Laura said. "He got dragged into advocacy because of my job. I turned into such an advocate, and I've met a lot of people who have a child or a spouse with LD. Over the years, he's been really great when he felt there was an opportunity to talk to a father about what is going on with that man's son or daughter. He'll tell them not to sweep it under the rug or make the child worry and wonder. He tells them, 'They need you to give them the help they need.'"

"Do they listen?" I asked.

"I think it helps," Kimo said. "It blunts the pain. If you tell them there is something specific that is wrong and that it can be diagnosed and there are ways to compensate, and it will help the child not feel stupid. The child isn't dumb. They have different strengths. You need to catch them doing something good."

"And the last thing I'd say is we also have a sense of humor about it all," Laura said. "That's really important."

ISLANDS OF COMPETENCE

An interview with Dr. Robert Brooks

*D*r. Robert Brooks is one of today's leading speakers and authors on the themes of resilience, motivation, school climate, a positive work environment, and family relationships. During the past thirty-five years, he has presented nationally and internationally to thousands of parents, educators, mental health professionals, and business people and is the author or co-author of fifteen books, many focusing on the issue of resilience and about the impact LD can have on social-emotional adjustment and family functioning, particularly during adolescence and the early adult years. I first met Dr. Brooks when he was a member of the Professional Advisory Board of the National Center for Learning Disabilities. I've heard him speak many times and have always been so impressed with his knowledge and his ability to share this knowledge in a warm and humorous way.

I started off by asking Dr. Brooks if he sees couples whose children have LD.

"Oh, I've seen many over the years. I don't see as many now because most of my work involves giving workshops and writing. But even in the workshops, I get a lot of questions from parents of children with special needs."

"Which challenge is brought up the most in these discussions?"

"It really varies from family to family. There are a few common themes that come up. For some families, the greatest need is simply to understand what their child's problem is. When we use terms such as 'learning disability' or 'learning difference,' what does that actually mean? Or what does ADHD mean? I spend a lot of time reviewing the definitions with them. Parents also ask what causes the problems their child is facing. They wonder if it is caused by their parenting or if it is genetics. Another concern for most families is to learn the kinds of strategies and programs that will most help their child, and if those programs are available. And finally, once parents come to accept their child has difficulties (which most do to a greater or lesser extent), they then want me as a therapist to be what I refer to as a 'futurist'. They know the problems exist, but the big worry is what the future holds for their child, especially as the child begins to reach adulthood. That worry lends itself to asking about those programs and services that are likely to help a child at this point so the future will be less stressful and challenging."

"When you said the parents may not fully understand what LD involves, is this before or after a diagnostic evaluation?" I asked.

"It can be both before and after the diagnosis," said Dr. Brooks. "To give you an example, if parents come in and their child has a physical disability or severe asthma, the problem or diagnosis seems much more clear-cut. But with the hidden disabilities such as LD, the situation may not be as clear. Sometimes parents will say things like 'if my child wanted to, he could work harder and do better', or 'my child is not motivated'. They may not really understand the extent to which the child has problems that are interfering with the ability to learn more effectively or to have better social skills. I have also seen parents whose child may have had a diagnostic workup but continue to have difficulty comprehending what is going on. They may come in and say, 'I'm still not certain what sensory integration problems mean'. They don't understand the terms that some professionals use to describe their child's problems.

"One of the things I learned to do in my clinical practice is to appreciate that a lot of time must be set aside both before and after the evaluation of their child to explain to parents the meaning of different terms and concepts. I have known some parents who became more frightened by the reports they read because they did not understand the descriptions that were used. I also believe that it is important to review the findings with the child. At the beginning of my career, I'd see a child for six or seven hours of testing and afterward meet with the parents and explain things thoroughly, but sometimes I felt I didn't do such a good job meeting with the child. That became a very important part of the diagnostic process, as was having a meeting with the child and the parents together after the evaluation. Speaking directly to the child also helped me learn not to use too much jargon. I had to speak in terms that the child understood, and parents often found that helpful as well. I also started to say very openly to parents, 'If there is any feedback that I give you that does not sound like your child, please let me know immediately. It's not that you're right and I'm wrong, or vice versa.' If there was a difference in the way I saw the child and the way the parents saw the child, I turned it into problem-solving and I would say, 'Now we have to figure out why some of what I bring up may seem different from what you observe because our main goal is to understand your child and the services your child requires.'

"I also said something with a number of parents that I felt was very important, namely, 'If at any time, anything I say seems to be critical of how you've handled your child's difficulties in the past, please let me know because I'm not here to be critical at all. I'm here to work closely with you to figure out what we can learn from past interventions that will help us in future interventions.' Many parents were already feeling judged when they came in to see me. They would tell me they felt their parenting was being judged anytime they went to a school meeting, especially when the discussion turned to their child's learning or attention or behavioral problems."

"Were these parents still thinking it was their own parenting skills that caused the problems?" I asked.

"Oh yeah! And you know what? When I first started as a psychologist, not so much was known about LD, so many well-meaning people fell into the trap of blaming parents. I actually heard other professionals in a school setting say, 'I wonder what these parents are doing wrong,' so that was why it was important for me to openly talk with parents about my not being perceived as critical of their parenting. One of my goals is always to help parents feel they are not being judged but, rather to offer support and empower them to help their child."

"Let's move on to couples who may be having a difficult time, both with each other and with the diagnosis," I said. "How should a couple handle differences in emotional responses?"

"That is an excellent question and it comes up a lot. Years ago I saw a child for an evaluation who clearly had learning disabilities. When I went over the evaluation with the parents, the mother started to cry. I felt they were tears of – not joy, but tears of acceptance or maybe relief. But when I asked her about it, she said, 'This just confirms that I'm to blame.' I was surprised, but then she told me that several family members had learning disabilities. She herself did not have LD, but she felt her genes had caused the learning problems and she was to blame. I had to do a lot of work with that couple and especially the mother to convince her that her parenting was fine and that she could no more control the genetic component of LD than she could control the color of her child's hair. LD does run in families, but hopefully, that should not result in parents taking on more and more blame. My work with this mother was to say, 'You had no control over your daughter having LD, but there are things you *do* have control over such as identifying and securing the services your child will need.' That was a major goal of my work with this mother in terms of her coping more effectively and becoming more resilient. Resilient people, when faced with difficult situations, do not blame the situation, they do not blame other people and they do not blame themselves. Instead, their mindset is to ask what they can do to help the situation. They adopt a proactive approach. Unfortunately some people spend too much time asking 'why me?' or 'why my child?' which is a normal response when parents find out their child has LD, but after the 'why me?' questions are asked, it's important to focus on what we can control. A boy once asked me, 'Why did God choose me to be the one with ADHD?' If a child has that belief, it can quickly turn into a victim mentality. I said to him, 'The answer to that is difficult to know, but the important thing is now that we know you have ADHD, there are things we can do to help you learn more effectively.' A major part of the strength-based model I use when working with parents is to explore the steps they can take once they know their child has a particular problem. It's quite common for many parents to get even more depressed and anxious when they are given a diagnosis, even though it may help clarify what's been going on."

"Think about the years that can be wasted with self-blame and denial," I said. "We once met a woman who had a daughter in her forties, and she told us she knew her daughter had LD because she smoked when she was pregnant. She had been carrying feelings of blame and guilt for forty years. "

"At least she was able tell you that," said Dr. Brooks. "There are people who never share those kinds of feelings or thoughts with anyone."

"It was a whispered share."

"It's very painful," he said. "It was the same with the woman who blamed herself because LD ran in her family. All too often, the child becomes the diagnosis. What I mean is that we only focus on the child's difficulties and lose sight of the child's strengths. To change this perspective I started to use a metaphor in my work, especially in my meetings with teachers and parents. After I'd heard about some of the problems, I would ask them to tell me what they saw as their child's strengths or what I called the child's *islands of competence*. I felt that we had to move the focus away from the child's difficulties. I have seen too many IEP plans that are primarily 'fix-it' plans, emphasizing the child's "deficits." The reality is that we will never truly touch the heart, soul, and spirit of children unless we can identify, reinforce, and use their islands of competence. A focus on strengths is not meant to minimize or deny the problems, but rather to look at what the child can do as opposed to what the child can't do. This outlook led me to develop and implement strength-based interventions with kids with learning and attentional problems and to recommend similar kinds of interventions when I met with parents and teachers."

"In what way?" I asked.

"To give an example, I was referred a high school girl who was struggling with learning and social skills problems. I asked her directly what she liked to do and what she thought she did well. I use these kinds of questions with all kids. A number reply, 'I don't know.' If they do respond with those words, I turn their 'I don't know' into a therapeutic task by saying, 'Then that's something we really have to figure out.' But this girl, without hesitating, said: 'I sometimes have trouble with kids my own age, but I love to teach younger kids.' What she meant by this was to play with them or teach them numbers and letters. I asked her parents what they saw as their daughter's strengths and their answer was parallel to hers. They said she's the pied-piper of the neighborhood, and though she may have some problems, she was also very responsible and that other parents loved her to babysit. So I went to the school and identified this island of competence and asked how we could use it.

"The teachers were intrigued by how best to use this particular island of competence and they developed a wonderful plan. There happened to be a nursery school right next to the high school and the teachers designed a class for her. They called it Child Development. She went to the nursery school four days a week, observing the young children and writing her observations about their behavior. One of the teachers was also the advisor to the high school newspaper and invited this girl to write an article, which she did with this teacher's help. So she's not only being assisted with her writing, but she's also 'published.' Kids her age who normally wouldn't approach her, came up to her and complimented her. That is an example of adults skillfully using a child or adolescent's island of competence. Equally important in my therapeutic approach, I began to ask the parents of children I was seeing in therapy what they viewed as their own strengths and interests. Some parents, in their quest to help their child, had given up some of their own interests and strengths because all their time was consumed with finding the best services for their child."

"We've talked to some mothers who said they wished they had an equal partner in this, or a partner who was more supportive. I don't know if you've found that."

"Oh yes, all the time," said Dr. Brooks. "One partner, usually the mother, is often the main person involved. In my clinical practice, I always inform parents that we're going to look at the ideal of what their child needs from them, but that I also respect how busy everyone is. I understand they don't have twenty extra hours in a week so we have to consider what is realistically possible for both parents. When I word it that way, I've often had mothers who say they don't think their husband can be of much help, but interestingly, after I've talked to the fathers directly of the importance of their role and the things they might do, some of those wives have been pleasantly surprised that their husbands actually can be of more help than they anticipated."

"What were some of the things you would suggest the father could do?" I asked.

"There was one father who felt he had to get to work very early and the mother was concerned because the mornings in their house were very hectic. This father changed his schedule so that a couple of days a week he would go in a little later and be available to assist at home in the morning. Even a couple mornings a week made a very positive difference. On the weekend this same father made certain he spent more time with the kids. In another example, there was a very athletic father who had a boy who wasn't athletic at all and had learning problems. In a session with me, the father said he wished his son would be more interested in sports. We talked a lot about it and I certainly empathized with him, but I also said, 'but that's not your son'. The father said he didn't know how to connect with the boy. I asked him what he thought was the boy's island of competence, and he said his son loved to draw and do artwork. I said if that were his son's island of competence, he had to figure out a way to relate to his son by using this strength. What happened was this: the father enrolled both him and his son in an art class in one of the museums in Boston."

"What a great guy," I said.

"Yes, he is. He called me after the first art lesson and said, 'I never realized what a pleasure it would be to see my son so happy doing something.'"

I told Dr. Brooks about a woman I met who told me she was sick of going to school meetings when all the teachers and administrators did was focus on the negative and never said anything positive.

"I could spend an hour on this topic," he said. "I give a lot of workshops for teachers. I advise them to look for the islands of competence in the kids and that they really have to communicate to parents that they are aware of the child's strengths. I have read psychological and educational reports that are twenty-five pages long and what I sometimes see is that the child gets lost under an avalanche of test scores and numbers and it's nearly impossible to discover if that child has any strengths. My suggestion would be that any IEP or treatment plan start by listing the child's strengths. I once went to a meeting where a school psychologist described a child as 'empty inside.' The parents were stunned. I asked him what he meant by 'empty' and he couldn't even explain it. As a result, the parents could not listen to anything else that psychologist said that day. The child was not empty. He had a lot of feelings but may not always have shown them. But the lesson here is that even one or two words can make a difference in how we perceive children, both negative and positive."

"Some of the mothers we've talked to don't need a whole lot from their partners," I said. "Sometimes the simple acknowledgement that the partner understands how difficult things are can be a huge help."

"Oh, what a lovely comment," said Dr. Brooks. "It's so important to validate another person's perception. I remember speaking once with a doctor and his wife. As a doctor, the husband was accustomed to prescribing things. In a meeting with him and his wife, she said, 'When I bring up something, I don't necessarily want you to prescribe an action for me. I only want to feel you understand what I'm going through. That's why I'm bringing it up. I want you to be a partner in this.' It was a very moving comment because she felt that if she brought up any concerns, her husband would immediately go over a list of what she could do to remedy these concerns, though the emotional part was absent. She attended IEP meetings, she met with the teachers, she was the main contact person. The father would go to school conferences, but the reality was that this mother bore most of the responsibilities when it came to their child with LD. All she really wanted and needed was for her husband to say that he appreciated all of her efforts on behalf of their child."

"We will undoubtedly have readers who do not or cannot go to therapy with their partners. What would we say to a mother who is in this situation? Or we could reverse it and ask what we would say to a father in this situation."

"I hope you do speak to both because I have definitely seen situations where the father takes the main role."

"Oh yes, we have too," I said. "But let's say it's a mother who is in a situation where she doesn't have a supportive partner. She loves him, but their having a child with LD had consumed her life. How does she approach him? What would she say?"

"In almost all of my books about resilience, I have a chapter about empathic communication," said Dr. Brooks. "What I mean by empathic communication is this: in my workshops, I ask people the following two main questions, and it doesn't matter whether I'm speaking with parents, therapists, or teachers. One question is, 'In anything I say or do, what do I hope to accomplish?' So let's say it's a wife thinking about her husband. She would say to herself, 'in anything I say or do, what do I really want to accomplish with my husband?' For example, the woman married to the doctor — all she really wanted to accomplish was for him to really hear what she was going through. The second question is this: 'Am I saying or doing things in a way in which the other person will be most likely to hear me and respond to me constructively?' To give an example involving children, teachers or parents will often try to motivate kids with learning or attention problems by saying 'Try harder, you can do it if you want to do it.' Yet, that statement almost always backfires. When I ask many adults with learning problems to tell me the least useful advice they ever received, it is not unusual for them to respond, 'When I was told to try harder or that I could do it if I really wanted to.' So look at the disconnect. Your goal is to motivate the child, and even though you're saying it in a caring way, it may be perceived as being judgmental or accusatory. It is likely to lead the child to become more angry and defensive. So now let's look at the husband and wife relationship. It's important to present something in a way that allows the other person to really hear it. That's why I tell people right up front to let me know if I say anything that doesn't fit with their understanding of their child, or if I say anything that sounds critical. I want them to be in a receptive mode to hear the message. I've seen communication difficulties in many couples. For those who are not seeing a therapist, these difficulties can exist for many years, causing a great deal of tension."

"What advice would you give them?"

"There are a couple of things I could say. They may sound obvious, but they're important. The first is, do not get into a major discussion or make major decisions when you are both angry. You've got to find an appropriate, calm time for constructive dialogue to take place. Some say they can't find the time, and I tell them they are wasting *more* time if they don't find the *right* time. It's like that wife said earlier, 'I don't want you to give me a list of things I have to do. I just want you to understand.' In the same way we want teachers to say positive things about children, it's important for parents to say positive things about each other. The mother could say, 'I know you're really concerned about our kids. One of them has some significant learning problems, and I really feel we have to talk about how we can support each other and what we can do.' There is research that indicates how the use of certain words such as 'we' and 'together' brings people closer together. Obviously, these words won't be effective if said in a dishonest way. What we want to do is create an atmosphere of cooperation.

"So even if parents are not seeing a therapist, they should ask these questions of themselves: How do we approach each other? Is it a calm time? Do I have a clear idea of what I would like to accomplish? If the wife says, 'I know you don't necessarily think our child has LD and that he's just being lazy, but in fact he *is* struggling and here are some things that I think can be helpful.' You turn the conversation into a problem-solving discussion and you also validate the partner's feelings. I've said to mothers that there is nothing wrong in saying to their husband 'I know you see this problem differently than I do, but we have to try to find some common ground.'

"Another favorite strategy when I work with parents and teachers is to use what psychologists call 'joining techniques.' One of my favorite joining techniques is the following: you may disagree 90% with someone about a particular topic, but find the 10% you agree on and begin working on that. Here's an example: there was a teacher who thought that a lot of kids with LD could do better if they 'tried harder.' She talked to me about one of my patients and she said, 'I want this student to be more responsible and accountable for his own learning and behavior.' I said, 'You know what? So do I.' I was joining her goals. I then said, 'I think we have some of the same goals, but where we may not be in agreement is the best way to achieve these goals.' After I said we had the same primary goals, this teacher was much more receptive to considering different strategies we might use. The same dynamic can occur between parents. A joining technique between a husband and wife is to ask, 'What do you want for our son or daughter?' Put aside the diagnosis. Ask what the other wants for the child. Invariably, they'll say they want their child to be more responsible or do better in school. Both parents can usually agree on that. And if that is the goal, then you have to start looking at some of the best ways of reaching that goal."

"What about the mother who doesn't feel she has a supportive husband, when, in fact, the reality is that she has become someone who is so completely obsessed with the child's situation, she will never feel she has enough support, no matter what he does? She doesn't talk about anything else, she doesn't think about anything else. She is consumed by the child's learning situation and probably brings it up all the time. You can see the husband's side in this situation. He wants a break from it once in a while."

"I remember working with a mother like that," said Dr. Brooks. "The pre-IEP conference took three hours because of the mother's constant questions and criticisms. And that was just the pre-IEP conference! The IEP conference itself was nearly four hours long. The mother went over every single detail, far beyond what was necessary. In this case, the mother's obsession with the child was keeping her from dealing with issues in the marriage. Once the child was getting the services she needed, some obvious tension appeared in the marriage. There was tension before, but it was always pushed to the background because of the focus on the child's situation. But let's say this is not the case. Let's say the mother is so worried about her child that she can't sleep and she's filled with anxiety — this is the time to seek counseling. There is no hard and fast rule about when to seek counseling, but I will say this: if you're even wondering about it, the time has come to explore the possibility. I don't believe everyone needs therapy, but I do believe that even obtaining a one or two session consultation with a clinician who knows about families with children with special needs can ease some of the anxiety. So if the situation with your child is taking all of your energy and you're overly anxious, I have no hesitation in saying you should contact a clinician. But make certain it is someone with some expertise in working with families with children with special needs."

"I can think of two situations where we interviewed mothers for books and didn't end up using them because they were so over the top with their anger and obsessions. I got the sense both times that there were other issues in the marriage that was causing this. The marriage was on the rocks in others ways, and they were focusing on the LD, the teachers, and the schools to deflect from the other serious problems."

"I've seen that a number of times, similar to the example of the mother I just discussed" said Dr. Brooks. "There are people who are upset and anxious and have good reasons to be. But what can also happen is that you have one partner who is obsessed, whether it's the mother or father, and then, after a while, the other one is going to become quite upset over this obsession."

"You don't want to listen to it all the time," I said.

"I agree. Imagine if you're in a house where 100% of the discussion is related to your child's learning problems and educational program, and then all that anger gets deflected to the teachers or the program. It can be very tiring."

"Another issue that comes up is the financial aspect of all this," I said. "It can be very expensive and become something of a financial burden. Of course, the first thing parents should do is approach the school to see what services are provided (or that the school *must* provide). Outside services can really be a burden. Both parents can have jobs and do their best, but there are always demands for more tutors and testing and therapy. That can cause tension too."

"Finances are a very big issue. Some parents have told me they had hoped to save for their child's college, but all that money was being used for the kid's services now. And sad to say, there are also some who say, 'I honestly wish I could do more but I have to be realistic. I can't go into debt because that would cause even more problems.' And they're right about that, though most of these parents feel terrible that they can't afford to provide their child with what they consider to be the best possible services. They feel they are letting their kid down, but I tell parents they must be realistic. In the best of all possible worlds, all these services would be available to all, but schools can only provide so much. Some of my work with parents is to sit down with them and review what they can realistically afford, to set priorities, and then find out what the school can adequately provide. For parents to be totally exhausted by having two or three jobs is not going to help the situation, so it's a real balancing act."

I told Dr. Brooks that we have met some parents who tell us there is a 'cocooning' of the family because a child has a disability and is disruptive and causes problems in public. "The family tends to withdraw and isolate themselves," I said.

"I've seen that dynamic with kids with significant impulse control problems or with kids on the autism spectrum. Some may just explode in public. I remember reading about a family who was suing their church. They had a young adolescent on the lower level of the autism spectrum, and he would suddenly start screaming during church services. They were asked not to bring him, and they felt that if they couldn't bring him to church, where could they bring him? They wished people would be more understanding, but I also understood the church's point of view. The kid would start screaming for no reason. The question then becomes what can you do as a family? There are no easy solutions. There are things that families can do when one of their children cannot be controlled. One of the parents can take the other siblings out to the restaurant while the other parent stays at home with the child with behavior problems. It's not the best solution, obviously and should only be used when all else fails in terms of dealing with the behavior problems in public. But we also have to be careful that the siblings without disabilities don't suffer too much. I've also spoken with some families where they have support, either close friends or grandparents who take out the children who are not going to cause the problems or they stay at home with the difficult child while the parents take the others out. The bottom line is this: there is no easy solution. I've always said – especially with an explosive child or one on the lower end of the autism spectrum who is going to be very difficult to manage – if the child is with a large group of people who know him really well, such as an extended family, many people just accept that is the way he will be. It's easier if it's outdoors at a barbecue, for instance. In that case, I would suggest the parents carefully select the situations where the child can be involved with people who know him and accept him for who he is."

"This all ties into the sibling issues too," I said. "In this situation children without the disability can start to feel neglected, whether they are or not."

"In the course of my career, I began to include siblings much more in my work with families who had a child with special needs. I wanted to establish a relationship with the siblings and see from their perspective the impact of having a brother or sister with a disability — and that impact can be observed in many situations. I've had siblings who've said 'we can't invite friends over because our brother acts so wild,' or 'she is an embarrassment in school. I wish she didn't have the same last name I do.' And then of course there is the dynamic in which siblings think they are being treated unfairly. I remember one situation where the girl in the family was a superstar student and the younger brother had learning problems. The mother called me one day nearly in hysterics because the daughter came home with a report card with two Ds and two Fs. We had an emergency meeting. The girl came into the meeting and said, 'So finally there is some attention being paid to me.' I said maybe we can get your parents to pay attention while you still do your work, and she laughed and agreed. That was the only semester she did poorly. It is important for parents as much as possible to set aside what I call 'special times' with each of their children. It is very powerful, though not always easy, to say 'there is going to be a time just with you.' It makes family life easier when children know there is going to be a time reserved just for them; the issue of fairness falls by the wayside a little."

"And that's the word they use — fairness," I said.

"Oh yes, it comes up all the time. When a kid says 'it's not fair,' I've told parents to not get defensive. When kids think things are not fair, it is very upsetting to them and so the best response is to ask them what they think you could do to make things fairer. You might not be able to do what they ask, but you can at least listen. If you have an immediate, negative, kneejerk reaction about fairness, it won't help. Parents have told me that validating what a child says and even thanking them for bringing up the issue of fairness really helped."

"Do you have anything more you'd like to say?"

"I would like to stress once again that it's very important to never lose sight of making certain we can identify and reinforce our children's islands of competence. And we must never lose sight of what our own strengths are. Being a parent is one role we play in life, and it's a very important one. For those with a child with special needs, it can be even more time consuming than usual — but we also have to learn to take care of ourselves. I feel the same way about teachers. It's very important for them to take care of themselves as well. It's a real balancing act to raise and work with children with special needs while at the same time making certain not to neglect one's own emotional and physical well-being.

"And one final thought. I became interested in resilience in kids because there are many kids who may not do well as children but who turn out to be very happy and successful adults. Research has found that one of the things that helped children with LD become successful adults is they abandoned the victim role. They never asked 'why did I have to have LD?' Instead they said, 'I was born with LD, but how do I learn to compensate?' I believe that parents and other caregivers can help children to develop this outlook.

A MOTHER'S ADVICE

Now that both of my children are independent adults, and after years of being immersed in these issues as both parent and advocate, I feel confident in offering a little advice when it comes to sibling and family issues. This confidence has only come after the passing of years, with enough time to reflect and gain perspective and, hopefully, a little wisdom. As you have seen from some of the stories, one of the greatest obstacles parents face when it comes to sibling and family-related issues is to recognize and understand that it truly is an issue, and one that may be far more serious than first imagined.

Here is a summary of the main points touched upon in this book:

Acknowledge the Problem

By now, most parents know that raising a child with LD can become an all-consuming task. Dr. Horowitz calls this the "24/7 LD Alert." The urgency of this alert ebbs and flows with the years and the severity and duration of the problems that arise, but it never completely disappears. We can become obsessed. We can become so engrossed in the day to day issues that arise that we become single-minded in our efforts to "fix" things. There can be costs associated with this — in relationships, in time spent with a spouse or other children, or other family members and friends who may not "understand". As we have seen, in extreme cases, a parent becomes so wrapped up in the trials and tribulations brought on by the child with LD that the marriage ends in divorce.

The first step in alleviating or overcoming a problem is to acknowledge the problem in the first place. When it comes to sibling issues, the easiest way to do this is to talk to your child (or children) without LD. Sit down with him or her, just the two of you. Ask about any problems, or if there is any sense of unfairness or injustice. Your child may very well say "no." After all, that child lives with a sibling with LD and surely understands on some level that their brother or sister with LD needs a little more attention. But even if the child really does understand on some level, there will be other levels that are less rational that nag at them and tell them over and over that "you are being treated unfairly." It is that less rational feeling that you need to uncover and address, even if you think its not there, or if the child insists he or she is "fine".

The truth is, most children are fine. Most truly do understand the need for the extra attention lavished on their sibling, but that doesn't always make it easier to accept. What does make it easier to accept is a parent who takes the time to sit down and talk to them, one on one, and explain the exact nature of their brother's or sister's disability and to acknowledge truthfully that you, the parent, understand how frustrating it must be. At the same time, try not to over-promise and say things like, "It will never happen again. I will divide my time equally between you both from now on."

The reality is that you won't. You will try...for a while. You will make every effort to be as fair as possible and distribute your attention equally. But then you'll remember you have an appointment with the dyslexic child's doctor, and "I would love to come to your basketball game, but I really need to bring her to this appointment." School meetings intrude. Tutors demand your attention. The endless, sometimes futile, efforts to help your child with LD find and maintain friendships takes up the time you might have spent with your other child.

This is the reality for most parents and to deny it or promise it will not be that way leads only to more tension and frustration, with a measure of newly-added anger over the broken promise. Again — acknowledge there is a problem, and be honest when explaining your ability and/or inability to be as fair as you would wish.

We have also seen that communication is vital when tension arises in a marriage. If you have tried to explain your child's disability to a resistant partner to no avail, the time may come to explore professional help. This need not mean marriage counseling initially: it may be something as simple as inviting a pediatrician or educational professional to explain the learning disability in a clear, undeniable way to the husband or wife who remains in denial.

Determine the Type of Child

Siblings of children with LD behave in varying ways toward their brother or sister. Some react with anger and resentment. Some feel an obligation to compensate by becoming the perfect child. Some will try to act as a "third parent" and develop a domineering attitude.

Some siblings feel guilty or ashamed of bypassing their brother or sister in certain skills. They may feel they are doing something wrong by being able to do things their sibling cannot.

In our third book, *On Their Own*, a father of two sons put it this way when talking about his young son James and how he viewed his older disabled sibling Charlie: "James is five years younger than Charlie, and when James was growing up, Charlie was walking and talking and taller, so James was looking to him as someone to emulate. As time passed, Charlie's progression continued to be slow and James progressed beyond him. I think of it as James going from someone looking at his brother through his developmental windshield to looking at him in the rearview mirror."

Parents may also unconsciously reinforce these feelings of guilt by feeling that they must withhold praise for the non-disabled child for fear of hurting their special needs child. Do not be afraid to praise all your children for real accomplishments, and certainly do not be afraid to talk about the siblings' disability openly and honestly.

Here is that same father talking about how he had the discussion with James: "The first time I spoke to him about his brother's disability was when Charlie started playing in Special Olympics basketball. James came to the event and there were a large number of children there with Down syndrome. James looked at all these people who looked similar and asked if they were all brothers and sisters. I explained that it was a particular disability, and that it was an issue with their genes. I said, 'It's different than the one Charlie has, but he also has an issue with his genes. That's why his motor skills aren't as good as yours. It doesn't make him anything less than a wonderful human being, but his development has essentially come to a halt. So you are going to be doing things he will never be able to do, and be sure you don't ever give him any grief about it.' And he never has. He would never say something like, "Ha-ha, I can ride a bike and you can't.' It would never occur to him to say something like that."

Explain, Explain, Explain

After so many meetings with doctors, neurologists, school psychologists and teachers, you may feel you know every detail about your child's LD, and it's true — you may. However, it is all too easy to assume everyone else in your family has the same level of knowledge you do. But do they? Have you told yourself that your other children are too young to fully understand? Maybe you've decided to wait a year or two to tell them what is going on with their brother or sister. Maybe you're afraid to put any kind of "label" on the disability, for fear your other children might view their brother or sister differently, or that friends may bully and tease the child with special needs.

Personally, I don't think I ever worried about my son labeling his younger sister, but I certainly never felt any sense of urgency about telling him what was going on with her. I look back on this as a mistake in dealing with the sibling issue.

The failure to explain what is going on can really pile up the resentments among the non-disabled children. The non-disabled sibling's need for information about their sibling's disability is significant. Parents should share the information openly, the way the father mentioned above did with James about his disabled son Charlie. Without this information, the sibling will develop assumptions that are inaccurate and blown way out of proportion. So do your best, even if the diagnosis is still a little vague. Anything is better than silence.

Spending Time Together

Another helpful remedy for sibling jealousy is to break away, in a forceful way, from the endless, obsessive focus on the child with LD. Take a day, or a weekend, and plan to spend it with one of your children without LD. If you have more than one, do the same for each in turn (it's probably not a helpful idea to group them all together, thereby excluding the one with LD. The whole point of this is to instill a sense of inclusion and fairness.) Do something the child without LD really wants to do — a movie, a museum, a favorite store: it doesn't matter. This is that child's day and time with you, and the memories and good feelings engendered by this one simple act can last a lifetime.

In my case, when my son was about fifteen years old, he developed a great interest in movies and all things having to do with film. He had heard about an exhibition of movie posters in Washington D.C., and I decided to bring him there to see them. I hasten to confess that I did not consciously do this to counter-balance the time spent with my daughter, though surely I must have sensed that he would have loved the chance to do something he wanted to do without his sister tagging along, or even more, without me fretting and worrying whether or not Allegra was having a good time. We took the train to Washington, D.C. and went to the Smithsonian, where the movie posters — about five of them — were exhibited in a room the size of a small office. But he didn't care, and neither did I. He loved it. I loved it. We had taken the train together and had lunch, went to the exhibit, got back on the train where we had dinner and returned to New York in time for bed. It only lasted a single day but he still talks about it, all these years later.

Be a Parent, Not a Friend

If you have never seen *The Miracle Worker*, the story of Helen Keller and her teacher Annie Sullivan, you must rent it. All parents of a child with disabilities of any kind should watch this movie and learn from it.

Helen Keller fell victim to scarlet fever when she was a toddler and lost her hearing and her sight. By the time she was a young teenager, she lived in a world of darkness and silence, and her parents allowed her free, uncontrolled and destructive reign of the house. They felt they had no choice — and then the teacher Anne Sullivan enters the picture. She is forceful and, to the Kellers, needlessly tough, but she believes in Helen and is determined to break through and help her.

The story is gripping, especially as one of the greatest obstacles to Helen's progress is not her disability, but the person who most loves her — her mother.

Mrs. Keller cannot bear to watch Anne Sullivan's methods. It is so much easier and kinder, she thinks, to let Helen live as she is, without being challenged in such a difficult way.

Who do you think finally steps up and objects and insists they send Helen back to Anne? Yes — the sibling. Helen's brother. He has had enough of living in the shadow of his sister's disability. He knows she can make progress. He believes in his sister and that belief bears fruit in one of the most moving scenes in film history, when Helen makes the connection between words and objects.

Mrs. Keller loved her daughter, of that there is little doubt, but she couldn't bear the thought of anything happening that might hurt her or make her feel "less than" or challenge her. This is an extreme case, to be sure — but mothers, rent the movie. Think about your own ability to step back and let the challenges come when they need to come, and determine whether or not you should step in.

Love your child, but love wisely.

Listen AND Hear

Some children will not hide their sense of injustice. Some will bring it up endlessly, to the point of making everyone miserable. Others will be more level-headed about it. They may bring it up occasionally, either in a fit of anger or in a serious "please listen to me" tone. If that happens, this is the best time to really hear what your child is saying and to have the heart-to-heart talk. This is not always easy. I fully admit that I, like so many mothers, listened to my son's complaints but didn't really hear them.

I now advise parents to avoid any off-the-cuff unhelpfulness such as "maybe *you* would like to have disabilities for a change" and, instead, really try to listen, accept and understand your child's concern, even if you don't believe it is legitimate or has a basis in reality. The fact is, it is real to that child.

Encourage your children without LD to discuss their concerns and problems openly, and how they experience having a sibling with special needs. At the same time, don't let this go on to a point of absurdity. Allowing them to vent once in a while does not mean you have given them permission to do it every day, all day long. Once you have explained the situation, and really listened to the concerns, it is time for life to go on. It's a lesson learned, to live with a disabled brother or sister.

It may not seem that way at the time, but there truly are positive results. There used to be a term that I don't hear much these days — character-building. It's a good term when applied to siblings of children with any type of disability. Early on they learn that life is not perfect, and people are not perfect, and that sometimes we need to make allowances for human foibles and failings. They learn compassion. Sometimes this lesson is forced upon them. They resist for a while and may complain, but more often than not, that child will be the first to come to their disabled sibling's defense when necessary.

If you can help guide them through this challenging time in their life with patience and open sharing and, above all, by listening to them, you will have gone a long way toward helping them become that more caring and compassionate adult we all hope for in our children.

The Future and the non-LD Sibling

Siblings of an adult with LD often bear additional responsibilities toward their brother or sister, especially when they are long into adulthood and the parent is no longer there. Much of this depends upon the severity of the disability, of course, but even for those with mild LD or ADHD, the benefits of an extended family cannot be overstated. Losing a parent is a difficult time for everyone and there's no question the new responsibilities thrust upon the non-LD sibling can be burdensome or even threatening to someone with their own spouse and children to worry about. Some may feel they have suddenly acquired another child, possibly at the very moment when their own children are finally out on their own. They may even find themselves in the position of trying to promote independence in their LD sibling, while at the same time, figuring out when to step in and assume control — the same dilemma their parents faced every day. The situation is even more difficult if latent feelings of resentment and jealousy resurface. That's why I so vigorously advocate clearing the air of these old resentments long before it reaches this point.

Here are a few questions parents have asked about sibling relationships and what might be waiting for the non-LD Sibling down the road.

"When should I talk to my son and daughter about their eventual responsibilities toward their LD brother if something should happen to us, the parents?"

This depends on how old they are now. If your children are adults, now is as good a time as any. Undoubtedly, they'll have already come to some conclusions on their own.

In general, eighteen is an appropriate age. They are mature enough to understand the situation, yet still young enough to believe it won't happen right away. Discussing future responsibilities at an earlier age works if a parent believes their non-LD children have the maturity to understand.

I told Alessandro of his future responsibilities when he was young, around age thirteen. This may have been too young, but he handled it all quite well. Even so, I didn't burden him with it all at once or in a way that might have caused worry or fear about the immediate future. "I think you should know that eventually, long after you and Allegra are grown, there will come a time when I won't be able to take care of her anymore. You'll have to be the big brother then and take over for me. Can you do that for me?"

Of course he could. I knew that then and I still do, but in my mind, I knew he might also have to be her guardian, her friend and even her father. I didn't say all those additional words then for fear it would all be too much for a thirteen year old.

You know your children best. I believed thirteen was appropriate for Alessandro. You may feel eighteen or older is appropriate for your situation. I think in this case you should rely on your mother's instinct: you will know what is best.

"What can we do as a family to help ease the burden on the siblings?"

Information is vital. The worst thing to do is to put things off until its too late. Estate Planning is essential. (You can find quite a lot of information on this in my second book *On Their Own*, but I would like to touch upon a few items here that have less to do with lawyers and wills as much as with simple common sense and consideration.

Plan for emergencies by creating a Master File with all relevant information about the LD sibling. This File should be kept in a place known by all family members and, depending on the severity of the LD and nature of the sibling's dependence on family and others, should include things like the following:

MASTER FILE

- Names and numbers of the LD sibling's doctors, dentists, mental health professionals and the location of all medical records.
- Copy of health insurance card and policy number.
- Information on relevant government programs, such as Supplemental Social Security (SSI) or Vocational Rehabilitation.
- If the LD sibling lives in an Independent Living Center, be sure to include all relevant information.
- Copy of disabled sibling's Social Security number, Passport and, if applicable, driver's license.
- Employment-related information, such as the name and address of the LD sibling's employer, in case of an emergency.

Including so much information may seem a bit overdone, but it's surprising how many small details of a person's life remain unknown to their siblings.

EPILOGUE

~ A Message For Brothers and Sisters ~

*W*ith all this talk of resentments and eventual burdens placed on the non-LD sibling, we can easily lose sight of the positive effect of learning disabilities in the life of a family. A disability of any kind brings an element of compassion and acceptance into a family, and I have a message for the siblings. You, as brothers and sisters of an individual with special needs, grow up seeing that not all people have an easy path in life and that some must struggle on a daily basis, often without much positive result. You may feel anger at times, resentment, jealousy or even guilt, and that is all completely normal; but in addition it is quite possible that you feel a surge of pride when your disabled sibling achieves something, or sympathy when they fail, and overall, feelings of love and devotion.

I have seen you countless times...

You are the sister with a family of her own still taking the time to escort her brother to a social gathering.

You are the brother who makes room for his older sister at his own family's table during holidays to make sure she will not spend them alone.

You are the one looked to and relied upon for various things both large and small by your parents, even though they may not always thank you for it, or even say so directly – but trust me, they do indeed look to you. You are as much a part of their thoughts as your disabled sibling, and in many ways your presence alone is the thing that most allays your parents' fears for the future and allows them to sleep at night.

Like so many siblings of children with LD and related disorders, my son Alessandro has a heightened sense of compassion. As he says, "I believe that having a sister with a disability forced me into acceptance." He watched Allegra struggle every day and watched my often futile attempts to make everything better, and he learned that we are all imperfect, all human, with failures and shortcomings, some of our own making and some not.

In the last few years it has been a little difficult for Alessandro and Allegra to communicate on a regular basis because she is on one coast and he is on another. They eventually decided to do something about this and set aside time for a weekly phone call to catch up on what each has been up to.

This is extremely gratifying to me. As I mentioned earlier, when Alessandro turned thirteen, I told him he would have to take on the responsibility for his sister if anything ever happened to me. He accepted without a moment's hesitation, and I knew in my heart he meant it and would do the best job possible, but that didn't stop me from worrying. I worried that Allegra might spend much of her time alone, or without a meaningful relationship apart from her family.

And then, on March 24, 2011, I received a phone call from Allegra to tell me she was engaged. By this time, I suspected the news might be coming, as the young man, Josh, had already called me to ask for her hand in marriage – such a gentlemanly, old-fashioned and completely charming thing to do! I was so excited and happy for her I couldn't help but cry. It was a real fairy-tale ending for Allegra, and one that I hoped might happen but did not expect. I was relieved she would have someone in her life who truly loved her and respected her. I also realized that this would not be the end of her dependency on me, and there would be days where she still relies on me for advice and guidance.

I try not to hover. I try to give her as much independence and time with her husband that she needs. I realize that not every child with LD will have the same ending as Allegra, but I also realize there is always a possibility for this or similar triumphs to take place. But parents must continue to play the role of advocate day by day, year by year. Remember, too, that triumph need not be defined as a marriage, for triumph and success come in many forms, as do happiness and contentment. Whatever is right and good for your child, and the thing that makes them most happy is the real triumph. For Allegra, it was marrying Josh. It was what she truly wanted at this stage of her life.

When Alessandro heard the news about her engagement, he felt as happy as I did. I'm sure he was a little relieved too. The responsibility for my daughter's future would no longer fall solely upon his shoulders. That's not to say he won't still be involved. He will always be involved in his sister's life: he walked Allegra down the aisle at her wedding, but the chances of him walking out of Allegra's life are non-existent.

At the rehearsal dinner, he stood up and gave a toast. This is what he said: "In days like these, a love story like the one that begins tomorrow is one that should give us all great hope. It is a love story that says to me 'There is a God and He really cares.' When two people as kind and two people as caring as Josh and Allegra find each other and decide to spend their lives together, what else can you do but smile and think that this world isn't such a bad place after all? Now I happen to be very close to the leading lady in this love story, and she's not your every-day run-of-the-mill movie star. And you only have to know Allegra for a moment to appreciate her mesmerizing laugh. For me it's one of those go-to memories that makes me smile when I need to. But even with all those memoires and special moments, there has been the most amazing and gentle force that has come into your life, Allegra. And there is that vibrant twinkle in your eye. For a big brother, that's an amazing thing to see. One of my proudest moments will be walking you down the aisle tomorrow and putting your hand in Josh's."

ACKNOWLEDGEMENTS

There were so many parents, siblings and professionals who helped us with this book. We couldn't possibly have written it without their input. Their honesty, compassion and advocacy formed the heart of our story.

Sometimes it was quite painful for them, especially when they reviewed the manuscript and saw their words written down in black and white. One mother told us, "I cringe when I read my own story and I would love to soften it, but the fact is I told the truth, and I hope that truth will help others going through the same thing." I understand that completely: I also had a very difficult time seeing parts of my own story in print, but I have learned that, yes, it *does* help others get through some of the same challenges. We are so grateful to the mothers of the Craig School and Gateway School for their willingness to share their personal stories with us and with you. They are: Valerie, Rosemary, and Suzanne from Gateway, and Nancy, Kathy, Sally and Marla from the Craig School (and a special thanks to Marla for making all the arrangements). In addition, we would like to thank Debra and her son Mark, also from the Craig School.

Stephanie Thompson proved to be an invaluable resource: her insights and experiences inspired us in so many ways. Special thanks goes to Janie for her help with the homework chapter, to Lisa for her insight into the effects of LD on a relationship, and to Donna and her son Luka for sharing their stories in the chapter about twins. Laura and Kimo Kaloi visited us in our New York office to talk about their experiences as parents of a child with LD and the challenges faced when one of the parents also has LD, and we cannot thank them enough for their willingness to share the lessons learned and their heartfelt advice.

Young adult siblings of individuals with LD sometimes have a particularly difficult story to tell, especially those who felt their childhood was lived in the shadows of a brother or sister with special needs. We are grateful to Melanie, Jason, and Sarah for allowing us to share their emotional, and sometimes difficult, memories.

We also had invaluable input from professionals with years of experience in the field of LD and family relationships. Dr. Carol Eagle, Clinical Psychologist and Clinical Professor Emerita of Child Psychiatry and Behavioral Sciences at the Albert Einstein College of Medicine generously donated her time and expertise, as did Dr. Robert Brooks, Clinical Psychologist and author of numerous books focused on themes of resilience and motivation in children with special needs, as well as family relationships and school climate. I first met Dr. Brooks when he was a member of the Professional Advisory Board of the National Center for Learning Disabilities (NCLD). Also from NCLD, is Dr. Sheldon Horowitz, Director of Professional Services. Apart from being a long-time friend, Sheldon has been of enormous help with all of our books, unfailingly generous with his time, his expertise and advice, and most of all, his deep understanding and caring for all those with special needs.

Much love and thanks to Allegra and Alessandro for being such an inspiration, and for their ongoing willingness to allow their stories to inspire others.

We would also like to express our deepest gratitude to our agent, Susan Cohen. She has championed this book from first to last, has gone over every sentence with a fine-tooth comb, has offered insight and guidance, friendship, and most of all, unfaltering belief in the project when we most needed it.

Finally, we thank you — the reader — of this, and *all* our books. You are the reason we do this. Your stories touch us. Your experiences encourage us. Your courage and efforts to advocate for your children are an inspiration to us all.

ABOUT THE AUTHORS

Anne Ford served as Chairman of the Board of the National Center for Learning Disabilities (NCLD) from 1989 to 2001. During her term as Chair, she led the reorganization and broad expansion of NCLD, including establishing a presence in Washington, D.C., and organizing educational summits on learning disabilities in several regions of the United States. She has received many honors for her work in the field of learning disabilities, including the Lizette H. Sarnoff Award for Volunteer Service from the Albert Einstein College of Medicine. Leslie University has conferred upon her an Honorary Degree, Doctor of Humane Letters, for advocacy for people with learning disabilities. She is the author of the popular and inspirational book *Laughing Allegra*, about her experiences as the mother of a daughter with a learning disability, *On Their Own: Creating an Independent Future for Your Adult Child with Learning Disabilities and ADHD*, and A Special Mother: Getting Through the Early Days of a Child's Diagnosis of Learning Disabilities and Related Disorders. She continues to work on behalf of people with LD, appearing as a speaker at conferences and corporations and schools.

John-Richard Thompson is an award-winning playwright and novelist living in New York City. He is co-author of Anne Ford's *Laughing Allegra*, *On Their Own* and *A Special Mother*. For more information, visit his website www.j-rt.com.

For more visit:
www.anneford.net

Also by Anne Ford and John-Richard Thompson

LAUGHING ALLEGRA: The Inspiring Story of a Mother's Struggle and Triumph Raising a Daughter with Learning Disabilities

"Few books have moved me as much as *Laughing Allegra*...I cannot recommend a book more highly than this. Halfway through I found myself making lists of people who would enjoy it. I encourage you to pick it up — and then spread the word."

~ *Bookreporter.com*

"This poignant, intimate portrait opens an often hidden world and illuminates the many ways learning disabilities shape the lives of entire families."

~ *Publisher's Weekly*

"This smart and welcome book is a gift for all parents, not just those with children with learning disabilities...An insightful guide through the challenges and rewards of parenting."

~ Tom Brokaw

ON THEIR OWN: Creating an Independent Future for Your Adult Child with Learning Disabilities and ADHD

"With deep understanding of the worries that are universal to parents of children with disabilities, Anne Ford has managed to provide down-to-earth, practical advice on every area that affects and adult child's future and ability to live independently: school, work, social life, financial well-being."

~ Sally Shaywitz, M.D., author of *Overcoming Dyslexia*

"With insight, candor, and optimism, this is a remarkably helpful book for parents and families who are dealing with the impact of learning disabilities as their children move up and out."

~James Wendorf, Executive Director
National Center for Learning Disabilities

A SPECIAL MOTHER: Getting Through the Early Days of a Child's Diagnosis of Learning Disabilities and Related Disorders

"Anne Ford has been a tireless advocate for children with learning disabilities. In this valuable book, she tells her own story and the stories of other mothers who might never have known about each other and might have assumed, as I did, that their situation was unique. If, in the earliest stages of understanding our child has a learning disability, we are able to recognize the signs, ask the right questions, seek help in the right places, we — and our children — might be spared some of the inevitable pain of this diagnosis."

~ Judy Woodruff
News Anchor, PBS NewsHour

Printed in Great Britain
by Amazon